Endorsements

I had the privilege of becoming personal friends with Dwain and Amy Miller. They both enriched and blessed Susan's and my life greatly. We will forever value the time of friendship that we had with Amy. We celebrate her graduation into Life more abundant but miss her dearly.

In the reading of this book, we remember the times we sat with Dwain and Amy and talked about their journey. Their hope was that the words on these pages would help the readers. Amy's eyes would fire up and her passion would be displayed. Dwain has completed a difficult task in finishing this book and fulfilling Amy's dream. As always Dwain has brought forth the clear truth that can make people free. I honor their work but honor my friend greatly in completing this task. As the reader you will find words on these pages that challenge, words that encourage, and words that will heal. As you read it ask Holy Spirit to burden your heart of someone that needs to read it and receive from God His love and healing. The work of being obedient and completing this book will provide a life-giving experience to many. Dwain, my friend, thank you for the honor of running with you. This book is a job well done.

Clay Nash
Minister/Author
Clay Nash Ministries
The Ark in Arkansas

Betrayal is an FYI book on never quitting. A masterpiece of incredible stories that are unbelievably informative about the interweaving of lives and purpose. A survival handbook. A road map for anyone on the journey of what seems in that moment...an impossible recovery from life's harsh extremities. The tenacity and new found desire to persevere you will gain by reading these testimonies will not just be...For Your Information...but...For Your Inspiration.

Bishop Steve McCuin
President
Steve McCuin Ministries Inc

******

I have watched Dr. Dwain Miller go from a polished, ambitious, and scholarly preacher to a broken, humble, and kingdom man of God. His late wife, Amy, was a "Grace" Christian very much like I am. She believed in what God has called me to do not only with her words but with her deeds. I will miss her and the love she and Dr. Miller shared. Although Dr. Miller has accomplished many things in ministry, my favorite qualities of his are the way he loves his children and grandchildren and the loyalty he has for his friends. He has been a forever friend to my father and a big brother to me. Betrayal is something that hurts deeply, but necessary in the Kingdom to go to the next level. This book will help you get past the hurt and return to the purpose God called you to.

Dr. Ronnie Phillips, Jr.
Lead Pastor - Abba's House
Founder of Ronnie Phillips Ministries International

Dr. Dwain Miller has blessed us with many powerful books. Never has he opened his heart and soul as he has in this new release, *Betrayal*.

Betrayal chronicles the moving story of surviving the betrayals that plague and often drive others out of the ministry. His surprising insight into David's betrayal by Jonathan is new revelation and extremely powerful.

Beyond all of that is the moving and heart wrenching journey that Amy, his late wife, endured in her life! In the last chapter, Amy tells her story and it is sadly true but in the end victorious.

This book is a tough and challenging read . Yet it is transformative to the soul of the reader. You can win over betrayal and disappointment….and you can demonstrate loyalty and love to those in your circle. This book is different so it can make a difference in our lives. May God bless you as you absorb the liberating truth of overcoming betrayal!

Dr. Ron Phillips Sr.
Pastor Emeritus of Abba's House
Hixson, TN
Apostle over Dr. Dwain Miller and The Edge Church

BETRAYAL

*Overcoming the Broken Trust of
A Covenant Companion by
Not Becoming What Was Done to You*

by

Dwain and Amy Miller

Copyright

Betrayal

Copyright © 2022 by Dwain and Amy Miller

All rights reserved. This book is protected by the copyright laws of the United States of America. This book may not be copied or reprinted for commercial gain or profit. The use of short quotations or occasional page copying for personal or group study is encouraged. Permission will be granted upon request from Dwain Miller.

Unless otherwise identified, Scripture quotations are taken from the Holy Bible, New International Version, Copyright 1973,1978,1984, 2011 International Bible Society. Used by permission of Zondervan. All rights reserved. Scripture quotations marked NKJV are taken from the New King James Version. Copyright 1982 by Thomas Nelson, Inc. Used by permission. Scripture quotations marked NLT are taken from the Holy Bible, New Living Translation, Copyright 1996, 2004, 2015. Used by permission of Tyndale House Publisher Inc., Wheaton, Illinois 60189. Scripture quotations marked AMP are taken from the Amplified Bible, Copyright 2015 by the Lockman Foundation, La Habra, CA 90631.

Contents

Introduction 1

Prologue 7

1. Where Was Jonathan? 11

2. The High Cost of Betrayal 29

3. Beware the Absalom Spirit! 43

4. How Did I End Up Here? 57

5. Guard Your Heart and Your Secrets 75

6. All Alone in a Dark Place 91

7. Betrayed by the Fear of Others 101

8. The Anatomy of a Betrayer 113

9. Looks Can Be Deceiving 127

10. Amy's Story 139

11. Dwain's Story 149

Dedication

To my Beautiful Baby Doll, Amy Ellenburg Miller

Amy was born July 3, 1967, and went to her heavenly home on October 19, 2021. This book contains her story of betrayal turned into triumph, which she penned herself. Her deepest desire was to help others find peace and healing through sharing her truth. She was my soulmate, and I will forever miss her.

BETRAYAL: be·tray·al /bəˈtrāəl / noun
The act of betraying someone or something or the fact of being betrayed: violation of a person's trust or confidence, of a moral standard, etc.

Introduction

My first recollection of Amy Ellenburg was in the preschool of Unity Baptist Church, where my father (Jerry Miller) pastored. We were four years old. We had been in the nursery together as babies, but my limited memory won't reach back that far. We also had the same babysitter and found ourselves playing in her yard, digging roads with spoons, and driving our Match Box cars through them.

My fondest memories of Amy were around age five; she became my "girlfriend," and I would chase her around her house, catch her, and kiss her. One day her mother, Barbara, saw me and called my mother, Mary Lou, to come to take me home. In church, we sat by each other next to her mother. Occasionally my father would stand me in a chair behind the pulpit, and I would sing *Put Your Hand in The Hand*, an old Gospel song. Upon finishing, I would return to her side. Many people commented how she looked at me with a glow of love during our marriage. I can tell you that she had that same glow at five. To quote the little rabbit from the movie Bambi, she was "twitterpated," and I must admit so was I.

Along with our best friend Jon Looney, we were the inaugural kindergarten class at Unity Baptist Church. While in kindergarten, her father (Earl "Son" Ellenburg) died at the age of 43. I won't go into details because she does so in her book portion. It was that event that I now know knitted my soul to hers. In my innocent way, I became her caretaker.

Betrayal

We continued our little innocent routine as boyfriend and girlfriend throughout the first grade. Amy took her first-grade class picture and wrote on the back, "I love you, Dwain Miller." We have a copy of the back of that picture framed in our house.

At the end of first grade, our family moved to White County, Arkansas. My father began pastoring another church and working in real estate and insurance. Amy and I stayed in touch by writing letters to each other. I can still hear her telling me, "When Momma would call out 'Amy, you've got a letter from Dwain,' my heart would skip a beat, and my stomach would fill with butterflies." But as time and distance do typically, we became involved with our lives away from each other and stopped writing.

When I was 14, dad moved to a small community named Humnoke, Arkansas. It was only about 45 minutes from DeWitt, Arkansas. That summer, in his well-drilling business, I went to DeWitt and worked for dad's best friend, Donald Ruffin (we all just knew him as Toad). Almost every day at lunch, he would give me five dollars and his work truck to buy me something to eat at Troy's Drive-In. I would pick up food there and make a beeline for Amy's house. We would sit outside and eat and talk. It was during that summer that we indeed became best friends. But, once again, I went back to Humnoke and got busy with my life, and she did the same, and we lost contact for two more years.

The summer before our junior year in high school, I ended a brief relationship with a girl in school. I thought *I wonder what Amy's doing?* I picked up the phone and asked her out on a date. She explained she had just ended a relationship of her own and agreed to allow me to take her out. Full of excitement, I drove to DeWitt, and we rode around town (which is about all there is to do in a small town). We went to Troy's Drive-In, sat in the parking lot, and talked. Her ex-boyfriend drove by with someone in the vehicle with him, and she made me follow them all night long. I knew that this wasn't going to work for me. When I dropped her off at home, like the good gentleman I was, I

Introduction

walked into her house, where I was promptly met by Barbara saying, "We go to bed at ten around here, Dwain, so it's time for you to leave." Amy walked me out under the carport and kissed me. She later admitted that it was almost like kissing her brother. That sure doesn't help a guy's self-esteem. So, I left that night knowing that both of us would move on to other relationships. I knew I loved her from five years of age, but she wasn't where I was.

Life would take us in different directions. We both married other people the summer after graduating from high school and had families. I also began preaching that summer.

Fast forward to 2007.

I preached a revival at First Assembly in DeWitt. She was on the praise team. It was then our friendship was reborn. Shortly after that, she went through a divorce and moved to Stuttgart, Arkansas. We often talked on the phone, and when in the area, I would stop by her work or apartment and talk. I know that wasn't the wisest thing to do, but we both were going through personal issues and prayed each other through them. I realize that many people won't believe this, but our relationship was platonic, and we indeed were just best friends.

Fast forward to 2017.

As God would have it, we both became single and started dating. Our Apostle, Dr. Ron Phillips met with us in March of 2018, counseled us, and gave us his blessing; he demanded that we get married. I never will forget him saying, "It's obvious to the whole world that you all are madly in love with each other, so you need to go ahead and get married." On April 14, 2018, my lifelong soul mate became my bride, and I can tell you that we had a four-year honeymoon.

In 2020 the pandemic hit, and we had no idea what was coming. Amy and I both contracted the dreaded disease in 2021, but as I recovered, she grew worse and ended up in the intensive care unit.

Betrayal

On October 19, 2021, Apostle Jacquie Tyre called and shared her vision of the glory cloud of God filling Amy's ICU room with His presence. I prayed it meant He was raising her up off her sick bed. I had gone to her room every day for 45 days, read Keith Moore's 101 healing scriptures to her body, and played worship music over her for the 30 minutes I was allowed to be there. I would kiss her forehead or cheek and say, "I love you, Beautiful! Tomorrow when I come, you're going to get off this ventilator and sit up in this bed!" With the thousands of prayers of faith, I truly believed that that would be the outcome. I received an update at 6:30 p.m., and all her vitals were stable. At 9:30 p.m., I received another call from a nurse practitioner who informed me that her blood pressure had dropped to 50 over 30, her heart rate was 30, and she had gone into renal failure. My son Ben drove me to Baptist Health in Little Rock, Arkansas. He and I were allowed to go into her room. Though her heart was still beating barely, and the vent was still breathing for her, I knew she was home. I decreed those 101 healing scriptures to her body one last time, kissed her on the lips, and said, "I love you, Beautiful! Thank you for making me the happiest man alive! I will see you soon in Heaven!" Her heart stopped, they unplugged the ventilator, she took three shallow breaths, and her body died. However, I knew she had long been escorted into the presence of Jesus before we ever arrived.

The following day I received word that another person had the same vision that Apostle Tyre had, except it was the night Amy went home. This time the glory cloud of God filled the room with the presence of the Lord, but this time Jesus walked in.

He asked Amy, "Do you like my presence?"

She replied. "Yes, very much so."

Jesus said, "You can stay, and I will show you the journey you will have to recover. Or you can come with me into the fullness of my presence."

Introduction

The hospital had told me it would take at least two years of very arduous rehabilitation for her to relearn everything after being on the ventilator for 38 days. I know in my heart that Jesus gave her a choice, and by her faith and free will, she chose to go with Him. I also know she decided to go with Him because she wouldn't have wanted to put me through that rehab journey, but I would have gladly done anything to have had her here in my life today! It gives me peace because I know the thousands of prayers prayed and the hundreds of scriptures and decrees made did not fail. There is one thing that God will not do, and that is to override a person's free will. Amy chose to go home with Jesus, and I don't blame her! I am a little ticked off, I admit jokingly, but I don't blame her.

There's a Garth Brooks song that best describes how I feel. It's called *The Dance*.

Looking back
On the memory of
The dance we shared
'Neath the stars above
For a moment
All the world was right
But how could I have known
That you'd ever say goodbye
And now I'm glad I didn't know
The way it all would end
The way it all would go
Our lives are better left to chance
I could have missed the pain
But I'd have had to miss the dance

Beautiful Amy, this book is part of your great legacy, along with the thousands of lives you touched with your unconditional love and acceptance of everyone! I LOVE YOU!

Prologue

In the Beginning

It was a cold winter night in a secluded cypress wood cabin where I sat alone in the dark, surrounded by cedar walls with a bottle of bourbon in one hand and a glass in the other. It was something that I'm not proud of, but I promised God I would be truthful about my story, and the truth is the truth. I was having one of those moments like Sonny, the Pentecostal preacher played by Robert Duvall in the film *The Apostle*, when he was talking to God, yelling, "Hey, God, it's Sonny! Please talk to me! I need you to explain some things to me!" That was precisely how I felt that night.

Earlier that day, I had been approached by the church's leadership that I had pastored for 24 years and was told to hand in my keys and clear out my things, and it was made clear what the consequences would be if I refused. In shock, caught off guard, I complied. At the time, my marriage had failed, and I was on a leave of absence under the supervision of our Apostle, Dr. Ron Phillips. He left me in place as pastor of the church that I founded in Little Rock but thought it best for me to step back from the main church. Unfortunately, rumors, innuendo, gossip, lies, and half-truths were spreading about me like wildfire. I had some personal failures in my life, but not to the extent or level that it was being told. When this occurred, Dr. Phillips was out of the country and advised the leadership to wait one week, and when he returned, he would visit with me and come to a resolution. However, that's not what happened. Against his direction, I was ousted. And, whether I deserved it or not, it was not the decision to make of those who made it. I felt the ultimate betrayal! My argument to God was that I had been there longer than any other in leadership. And that I didn't deserve how I was being treated, and they were out from under authority. I could go on and on, but you get the idea. Not only had my marriage failed, and the church I spent half of my life building ousted me without doing so biblically, but every ministry friend I thought I had, wouldn't answer a text or a call, except for two or three advisors.

As God and I had our moment, He said to me, "Are you finished?"

"Yes, Sir," I replied.

"Let me ask you a question," said God. "Where is Dwain? Where is the eighteen-year-old I called to preach? A boy who was so excited and inspired that he would preach on the street corner, witness to anyone who would stand still for five seconds and when an invitation came to preach, you didn't care if the church had five people or five hundred people. You didn't care if they could even pay your travel expenses. That Dwain was pure and preached for the passion of my call and not his agenda! Nowadays, you won't go preach if the pay isn't sufficient or the opportunity large enough."

At that moment, I became more broken than I've ever been. I wept and repented before God until my eyes swelled shut. Not only did I ask God to forgive me, but I forgave all those that I felt had wronged me, realizing that it wasn't them who had betrayed me, but me who had betrayed myself and all the people that looked to me as a leader. How did I betray them? I had become a professional preacher! I was in it for every reason but the right reason. I was using people to build my ministry, not using the ministry to build people.

In the end, I had become what had been done to me! I am here to tell you that God's love, grace, mercy, and forgiveness covered me like a warm blanket of His glory, and God began to heal me.

Not long after this event, I received a letter from a dear lady who watched me on Victory Television Network. She asked if I might come and share with her Bible study group in her home. She noted that there might be only eight of them, and if I couldn't come for such a small group, she would understand. I was more excited about that invitation than any I have ever received! It was the first step to the new me.

In this book, you will read of many of God's most choice servants who felt the pain of betrayal. You will see their heartbreak and pain in the midst of it and how they responded. How a man like King David realized that Jonathan, the man he made a covenant with, actually had betrayed him multiple times and, but for the hand of God, it would have cost him his life. When you read Psalms 41 and 55, you find the pain of that betrayal is almost too much for David to bear.

My beautiful wife, Amy, and I wrote about this subject because ALL of us will be betrayed—it's not a matter of if—but when. What we do with that betrayal will determine whether we live in promotion or pity for the rest of our lives. Whether we maximize our God-given potential or simply exist during our lifetime is based on our choices.

You will also read Amy's story, which I believe is the most remarkable story I've ever heard of overcoming overwhelming obstacles and turning your personal pain into opportunities to help others.

Our dearest friend, Apostle Clay Nash, always introduces us as "the ones who walk with a limp." This is very true. Our story is one of redemption, restoration, reconciliation, and reshaping for His Kingdom's purpose.

I issue you this warning: Stop here and read no further if you are religious. But if you need a second chance or have ever been betrayed, this book is for you.

1

Where Was Jonathan?

Betrayed by a friend

The saddest thing about betrayal is that it never comes from your enemies.

Unknown Author

Even my best friend, the one I trusted completely, the one who shared my food, has turned against me.

Psalm 41:9 NLT

At some point in our life, we will be betrayed.

It's not only a fact borne out in scripture but also proved in our human interactions. It shouldn't surprise anyone that Jesus was betrayed by someone close to him and warned us that we too should not be shocked when we are faced with similar circumstances. It's not a matter of if, but when. The key is what we do with the betrayal. It will either be our platform for promotion or become our gallows for destruction. John 13:21 says, "Now Jesus was deeply troubled, and he exclaimed, 'I tell you the truth, one of you will betray me!'"

Betrayal

The word betray means, "to hand over or to deliver over treacherously by way of betrayal, or to give away someone you are in covenant with, or to hand them over."

Aside from the Lord Jesus, no other figure in the Bible dealt with betrayal more than David.

Just read his lament, and you can feel the pain in his heart:

> *My heart pounds in my chest.*
> *The terror of death assaults me.*
> *Fear and trembling overwhelm me,*
> *and I can't stop shaking.*
> *Oh, that I had wings like a dove;*
> *then I would fly away and rest!*
> *I would fly far away*
> *to the quiet of the wilderness.*
> *Interlude*
> *How quickly I would escape—*
> *far from this wild storm of hatred.*
> *It is not an enemy who taunts me—*
> *I could bear that.*
> *It is not my foes who so arrogantly insult me—*
> *I could have hidden from them.*
> *Instead, it is you—my equal,*
> *my companion and close friend.*
>
> Psalm 55:4-8, 12-13 (NLT)

Who was David referring to in these verses? Who was the friend that he trusted in completely, the one who shared his food? Who was David talking about when he said, "Instead, it is you—my equal, my companion and close friend?"

I believe he was referring to Jonathan—David's covenant friend—and Jonathan's betrayal hurt more than if you had taken a sword and cut out his heart!

Where Was Jonathan?

If you have ever had a friend look at you in the eye and declare that they would never leave you or turn against you and they did, you know something of the pain David felt. You have to read to the end of the story to see that David finally figured out that Jonathan had indeed turned his back on him. The pain of Jonathan's betrayal never left his heart.

> *Life has taught me that you can't control someone's loyalty, no matter how good you are to them, doesn't mean that they will treat you the same. No matter how much they mean to you, doesn't mean that they will value you the same. Sometimes the people you love the most, turn out to be the people you can trust the least.*[1]
>
> Trent Shelton

We are introduced to Jonathan in 1 Samuel 13. There are many wonderful characteristics attributed to him. He was a man of faith, courage, vision, and unselfishness. He was the king's son, next in line to take the throne of his father. But storm clouds loomed over the nation of Israel. Darkness and despair were slowly enveloping the people, and they knew something had to change. Jonathan had enough spiritual insight to understand that David, not himself, would sit on the throne.

> *And he said to him, "Do not fear, for the hand of Saul my father shall not find you. You shall be king over Israel, and I shall be next to you. Even my father Saul knows that." So the two of them made a covenant before the LORD: and David stayed in the woods, and Johnathan went to his own house."*
>
> 1 Samuel 23:17-18 (NKJV)

---

[1] https://www.goodreads.com/quotes/7296140-life-has-taught-me-that-you-can-t-control-someone-s-loyalty accessed November 20, 2020.

But, in the end, Jonathan's real intentions would be revealed. It wouldn't take very long for the world to know that there was more to this story besides a covenant between the shepherd boy and the prince.

Consider the kind of covenant a betrayer makes. A betrayer's covenant is always based upon *what you can do for me* or *what's in it for me?* In Jonathan's case, it was a self-centered, me-first attitude.

Jonathan knew that his father's reign as king was over, and now he's voicing insincere platitudes to David. Why? Jonathan knows David will be the next king of Israel. Notice how he affirms David's soon-to-be promotion; "You shall be king over Israel, and I shall be next to you!" He's only looking out for himself, and not applauding David as God's choice for Israel.

Jonathan is saying, this covenant takes care of me and my family—it is my insurance policy for the future. He knows that in their culture the new king would kill all the previous king's descendants. Jonathan was saying, you'll be king, but I want your word that I will be your Prime Minister.

Every relationship has a starting point—David and Jonathan were no different. Look at how this relationship began.

> *Now when he had finished speaking to Saul, the soul of Jonathan was knit to the soul of David, and Jonathan loved him as his own soul. Saul took him that day, and would not let him go home to his father's house anymore. Then Jonathan and David made a covenant, because he loved him as his own soul. And Jonathan took off the robe that was on him and gave it to David, with his armor, even to his sword and his bow and his belt.*
>
> 1 Samuel 18:1-4 (NKJV)

A soul tie was formed in this covenant. The word *knit* in Hebrew is *qashar* which means, "to tie something together," thus two becoming one. It is the language used in the marriage covenant. Again, the covenant between David and Jonathan may or may not have been physical; however, it was deeply emotional and unhealthy. It was through this unhealthy, deeply emotional soul tie that Jonathan would manipulate the terms of the covenant with David to his advantage. Look at how Jonathan uses the covenant between the two and moves the language toward his personal well-being.

> *And you shall not only show me the kindness of the Lord while I still live, that I may not die; but you shall not cut off your kindness from my house forever, no, not when the Lord has cut off every one of the enemies of David from the face of the earth. So Jonathan made a covenant with the house of David, saying, "Let the Lord require it at the hand of David's enemies." Now Jonathan again caused David to vow, because he loved him; for he loved him as he loved his own soul.*
>
> *Then Jonathan said to David, "Go in peace, since we have both sworn in the name of the Lord, saying, 'May the Lord be between you and me, and between your descendants and my descendants, forever.'" So he arose and departed, and Jonathan went into the city.*
>
> 1 Samuel 20:14-17; 42 (NKJV)

Take a very close look at the terms of the covenant.

- 1 Samuel 18:1 "The soul of Jonathan was knit to the soul of David, and Jonathan loved him as his own soul."

The statement that Jonathan loved David "as his own soul" and that their souls were knit together, suggests that a very unhealthy infatuation was enabling Jonathan to direct the terms of their covenant to obtain self-preservation.

- 1 Samuel 23:17 "You shall be king over Israel, and I shall be next to you." Jonathan would be number two in command, thus preserving his livelihood and position in the nation.
- 1 Samuel 20:14-15 "Show me the kindness of the Lord while I still live, that I may not die; but you shall not cut off your kindness from my house forever." Notice the language of the covenant is all about Jonathan and his family being preserved.
- 1 Samuel 20:17 "Jonathan again caused David to vow... for he loved him as his own soul." Can you say, *Manipulation*! It's like Jonathan is saying, now you have to promise me—I mean it—promise me—I'm serious—give me your word. Notice the intensity with which Jonathan is pressing David for his own well-being.
- 1 Samuel 20:42 "May the Lord be between you and me, and between your descendants and my descendants forever." Now Jonathan brings the name of God into it. He's saying, you've got to swear on the name of the Lord that you will take care of me and my family.

I get it! The guy doesn't want to die, and he wants to maintain his lifestyle. But can you see the narcissism in this whole sham of a covenant? The real question is why couldn't David see through this attempt at self-preservation?

Why does a betrayer make that kind of covenant? It's very simple, to have complete control.

Jonathan used his father's rage and incessant desire to kill David to his advantage. Jonathan feels like he is in control and calling all the shots. He is in a win-win situation. If Saul kills David, then he's the king. If Saul loses, then Jonathan is Prime Minister. Either way, he wins.

Jonathan's narrative to David about Saul is packed full of lies and half-truths.

Where Was Jonathan?

Event One

> *Now Saul spoke to Jonathan his son and to all his servants, that they should kill David; but Jonathan, Saul's son, delighted greatly in David. So Jonathan told David, saying, "My father Saul seeks to kill you. Therefore please be on your guard until morning, and stay in a secret place and hide. And I will go out and stand beside my father in the field where you are, and I will speak with my father about you. Then what I observe, I will tell you." Thus Jonathan spoke well of David to Saul his father, and said to him, "Let not the king sin against his servant, against David, because he has not sinned against you, and because his works have been very good toward you. For he took his life in his hands and killed the Philistine, and the Lord brought about a great deliverance for all Israel. You saw it and rejoiced. Why then will you sin against innocent blood, to kill David without a cause?" So Saul heeded the voice of Jonathan, and Saul swore, "As the Lord lives, he shall not be killed." Then Jonathan called David, and Jonathan told him all these things. So Jonathan brought David to Saul, and he was in his presence as in times past. Then Saul sought to pin David to the wall with the spear, but he slipped away from Saul's presence; and he drove the spear into the wall. So David fled and escaped that night.*
>
> 1 Samuel 19: 1-7, 10 (NKJV)

If anyone knows Saul, it's Jonathan. He knows that his father cannot control his rage toward David. So, he devises a plan to give David a sense of security by manipulating his father with kind words about David. He knew that if David returns to Saul's presence it was only a matter of time before Saul snaps again. And he did.

Event Two

> *Then David fled from Naioth in Ramah, and went and said to Jonathan, "What have I done? What is my iniquity, and what is my sin before your father, that he seeks my life?" So Jonathan said to him, "By no means! You shall not die! Indeed, my father will do nothing either great or small without first telling me. And why should my father hide this thing from me? It is not so!" Then David took an oath again, and said, "Your father certainly knows that I have found favor in your eyes, and he has said, 'Do not let Jonathan know this, lest he be grieved.' But truly, as the Lord lives and as your soul lives, there is but a step between me and death." So Jonathan said to David, "Whatever you yourself desire, I will do it for you."*
>
> 1 Samuel 20:1-4 (NKJV)

Jonathan again manipulates and controls David. David's love and trust are fully committed to their covenant, so he believes Jonathan. Jonathan says, "By no means! You shall not die…my father will do nothing…without first telling me." Jonathan again gives David a false sense of security by embellishing his loyalty by saying, "Whatever you desire, I will do it for you." If that's true, then why be so vague about the whole situation. He should be saying, "David, Saul's out to kill you. Now you go hide and wait for the Lord's timing to put you in the office!" But he didn't. He's hedging his bets, hoping for a different outcome.

Event Three

> *Therefore you shall deal kindly with your servant, for you have brought your servant into a covenant of the Lord with you. Nevertheless, if there is iniquity in me, kill me yourself, for why should you bring me to your father?" But Jonathan said, "Far be it from you! For*

Where Was Jonathan?

> *if I knew certainly that evil was determined by my father to come upon you, then would I not tell you?"*
>
> 1 Samuel 20: 8-9 (NKJV)

David is saying, "This is no game! Why don't you kill me and bring me to your father?" Jonathan deflects once more and lies again, "Far be it from you! For if I knew certainly that evil was determined by my father to come upon you, then would I not tell you?" Wow! What manipulation! In essence he is saying, "You don't believe me! David, what have I ever done for you not to believe me? I am so hurt!" The insincerity of Jonathan is laughable if it weren't so serious.

Event Four

> *And he said to him, "Do not fear, for the hand of Saul my father shall not find you. You shall be king over Israel, and I shall be next to you. Even my father Saul knows that."*
>
> 1 Samuel 23: 17

That is an outright, blatant lie, Saul did find David. This brings us to the very crux of the issue within a betrayer's heart, and that is the betrayer's conspiracy.

Firstly, what does a betrayer's conspiracy look like? A betrayer works behind the scenes to remove their opposition and those that threaten what they want. Jonathan assured David, "Dad won't find you." But five times, Saul discovered David's whereabouts, and only Jonathan knew where he was. Let that sink in. David hid five times and Saul found him all five times; Jonathan is the only one who knew where David was.

Five times Saul finds David's whereabouts and only Jonathan knew where he was:

1. Saul heard that David and the men who were with him had been discovered. (1 Samuel 22:6)

2. And Saul was told that David had gone to Keilah. (1 Samuel 23:7)

3. Then it was told to Saul that David had escaped from Keilah. (1Samuel 23:13)

4. And when Saul heard that, He pursued David in the Wilderness of Maon. (1 Samuel 23:25)

5. It was told to him saying, "Take note! David is in the Wilderness of En Gedi." (1 Samuel 24:1)

Secondly, a betrayer's conspiracy is full of flattery to mask their motives. Listen again to Jonathan's insincere decree.

> *And he said to him, 'Do not fear, for the hand of Saul my father shall not find you. You shall be king over Israel, and I shall be next to you. Even my father Saul knows that.'*
>
> 1 Samuel 23:17 (NKJV)

Thirdly, and most importantly, a betrayer's conspiracy is always motivated by self-preservation. Repeatedly Jonathan stated, "I shall be next to you! You shall not cut off your kindness from my house forever." It is all about Jonathan. Jonathan wanted to be king, but he hedged his bets just in case David didn't die and made it to the throne. *If David lives, he spares my life, and my family and I keep my position as number two. David is king and I am prime minister.*

No wonder David said later in life.

> *Even my best friend, the one I trusted completely, the one who shared my food, has turned against me.*
>
> Psalm 41:9 (NLT)

> *It is not an enemy who taunts me—I could bear that. It is not my foes who so arrogantly insult me—I could have hidden from them. Instead, it is you—my equal, my companion and close friend.*
>
> Psalm 55: 12-13 (NLT)

Where Was Jonathan?

In the end, how did David respond to Jonathan's betrayal?

> *Now David said, 'Is there still anyone who is left of the house of Saul, that I may show him kindness for Jonathan's sake?'*
>
> 2 Samuel 9:1 (NKJV)

David kept the covenant with Jonathan's son, Mephibosheth.

> *Now David said, "Is there still anyone who is left of the house of Saul, that I may show him kindness for Jonathan's sake?"*
>
> *And there was a servant of the house of Saul whose name was Ziba. So when they had called him to David, the king said to him, "Are you Ziba?"*
>
> *He said, "At your service!"*
>
> *Then the king said, "Is there not still someone of the house of Saul, to whom I may show the kindness of God?"*
>
> *And Ziba said to the king, "There is still a son of Jonathan who is lame in his feet."*
>
> *So the king said to him, "Where is he?"*
>
> *And Ziba said to the king, "Indeed he is in the house of Machir the son of Ammiel, in Lo Debar."*
>
> *Then King David sent and brought him out of the house of Machir the son of Ammiel, from Lo Debar.*
>
> *Now when Mephibosheth the son of Jonathan, the son of Saul, had come to David, he fell on his face and prostrated himself. Then David said, "Mephibosheth?"*
>
> *And he answered, "Here is your servant!"*

So David said to him, "Do not fear, for I will surely show you kindness for Jonathan your father's sake, and will restore to you all the land of Saul your grandfather; and you shall eat bread at my table continually."

Then he bowed himself, and said, "What is your servant, that you should look upon such a dead dog as I?"

And the king called to Ziba, Saul's servant, and said to him, "I have given to your master's son all that belonged to Saul and to all his house. You therefore, and your sons and your servants, shall work the land for him, and you shall bring in the harvest, that your master's son may have food to eat. But Mephibosheth your master's son shall eat bread at my table always." Now Ziba had fifteen sons and twenty servants.

Then Ziba said to the king, "According to all that my lord the king has commanded his servant, so will your servant do."

"As for Mephibosheth," said the king, "he shall eat at my table like one of the king's sons." Mephibosheth had a young son whose name was Micha. And all who dwelt in the house of Ziba were servants of Mephibosheth. So Mephibosheth dwelt in Jerusalem, for he ate continually at the king's table. And he was lame in both his feet.

2 Samuel 9:1-13 (NKJV)

David did not allow Jonathan's breaking of the covenant to influence his decision to keep the covenant. Covenant meant more to David than revenge. David was more concerned about relationships than being right. He had a right to kill Mephibosheth, but instead, he gave him a permanent seat at his table. That sounds familiar to me. God had every right to punish me for my sin, but because of the covenant He made with His Son, he invited you and me to sit at His table forever. Hallelujah!

A Final Thought

One of the most disappointing things that I have learned in over 37 years of ministry is that there are very few real friends. My father, a pastor of more than 60 years, told me when I first started in ministry, "Son, when you get to the end of your life and ministry, if you have had five or six loyal and real friends, you will have been a rich man."

Over these years, I have made a covenant with many church members, elders, ministry leaders, and pastors. I can say without exaggeration or embellishment that almost all of them have betrayed me in one way or another. One of my true friends, Dr. Randy Caldwell, told me something—over a decade ago—that has proven true. He said, "Miller, when you become more of a liability than an asset to someone, or if you are no longer able to do something for them, a preacher will throw you away and lose your number so fast it'll make your head spin!"

You know what? He was right. Very few relationships are built on authentic principles like, "What can I do to serve you?" or "How can I love you and support you through this tragic time in your life?"

Proverbs 17:17 says, "A friend loves at all times, and a brother is born for a time of adversity." My experience has been that there are very few people who love like this.

In 2017 I went through a personal hell. Our ministry was at its peak. We had preached in some of the largest venues and conferences in America. Our television broadcast was at its highest ratings. Our income was unlike anything I ever dreamed of, and we had more invitations than we could fill. Then, a major disaster struck. I had hidden the fact that my marriage had been in trouble for over a decade. I had failed to get help, and as a result, my marriage failed. Rumors began to fly. The saddest and most heartbreaking events of my life were about to unfold. Men and women that I had made a covenant with, served with, and blessed began to talk about my situation to other ministers without knowing the truth about my situation. To this day, all but a handful of people who I was in covenant with have yet to sit with me, talk to me, or even endeavor to know the truth. People embraced rumor, innuendo, and their wild imaginations, rather than following the teachings of Matthew 18:15, and come to me directly and confront me in love. The principle that Paul taught in 1 Timothy 5:19 about entertaining an accusation against an elder, "except by two witnesses," was ignored. Yes, Dr. Randy Caldwell was prophetic when he said, "Miller when you become more of a liability than an asset, preachers will leave you." And, you know what, they didn't just leave; their gossip, phone calls to other ministries "warning them about my sin" all but destroyed our ministry. The saddest part of all of this was men and women that I had mentored, that I had served with, and laymen with whom I had been close confidants chose to listen to lies or half-truths and never once allowed me to share the whole truth with them. And, to this day, I haven't spoken to most of them. They just wrote me out of their lives as if I never existed.

In 2017, I lost what I now know were ministry acquaintances, not friends. I think I know a little of how David felt when he said in Psalm 41:9 (NLT), "Even my best friend, the one I trusted completely, the one who shared my food, has turned against me."

David was speaking of Jonathan in Psalm 41. He got to the end of his life and looked back to realize that Jonathan was riding his success for his self-preservation. I know exactly how he felt. People love you when you're on top, but the moment it looks like you might fall, those on your team and those fans in the stands will quickly survey the field for the next hottest team they can join.

I must say that my Apostle, Dr. Ron Phillips, stood by me, chastised me in love, disciplined me, and ultimately demonstrated to me what being a true friend and father is about. All the while demonstrating to me what unconditional love looks like. He likes to say, "I am hard to break up with," and he has indeed shown that to me.

My dear friend, Dr. Bob Vineyard, was one of the first voices I heard on the phone, and he said, "Brother, I don't throw anyone away!" In May of 2018, he invited my new wife, Amy, and me to minister with Dr. Ron Phillips and Dr. Tod Zeiger at his church. These men took a significant risk. They did receive much ridicule. But they allowed unconditional love and a real covenant relationship to override religious zealots in the end.

In March of 2019, I stood in front of Abba's House and publicly repented for a failed marriage. Under the correction and direction of our Pastor Dr. Ronnie Phillips Jr. and our Apostle Dr. Ron Phillips, Amy and I were publicly restored. At the end of the day, the Heavenly Father, Dr. Ron Phillips, Amy, and I are truly the only ones who know the truth, the whole truth, and nothing but the truth.

Along the way I learned something very valuable; I learned the difference between relational authority and covenantal authority. I learned this lesson in October of 2018, when Apostle Clay Nash, who was only an acquaintance at the time, sought me out and said, "Dwain Miller, the Holy Ghost has called me to be your friend. I don't want an explanation; I want to love you and be in a relationship with you." It was that event and his book on *Relational Authority* that transformed my life. You see, a covenant relationship can end when one party breaks the terms of the covenant. But a relationship based on proper biblical authority remains intact regardless of the conduct of either party. Why? Because it is based on the divine connectors: the unconditional love of the Father, the unmerited forgiveness of the blood of the Son, and the unrelenting mercy and grace of the Holy Spirit that heals all. This revelation revealed to me that I had been operating ignorantly under an illegitimate authority. I learned that true apostolic authority behaves like the father of the prodigal, running toward the swine-swilled sinner, not running from him. The blessing for Amy and me is that Apostle Clay and Susan Nash and Apostle Ron and Paulette Phillips ran toward us, not from us.

I have also learned how to be much more gracious and merciful to others. I have learned what it means to stand beside others who are damaged and wounded. I may have been deeply betrayed in this journey, but I found out what true loyalty is. I learned this from my faithful friend and brother, Bishop Steve McCuin, who reached out to me at my lowest moment

"You're not going to panic," he said. "And you're going to put your oar in the water and keep rowing! You are going to come to my building and film your television program and keep doing what God has called you to do!"

"I don't think I can pay you," I said.

"I didn't ask for payment. You are my brother, and I love you, and I believe in you, and God's not finished with you!"

Then he made the most profound statement to me.

"Dwain Miller, the only way the devil wins and you fail is if you quit doing what God created you to do!"

I have learned that the most authentic people in ministry are those who "walk with a limp," to quote Apostle Clay Nash. That's what God has raised up at our church in Little Rock; a loyal, loving congregation of people who are damaged but at the same time mature enough to focus on what matters.

In the end, because of my failure, I may have lost a church that I pastored for 24 years, hundreds of ministry opportunities, and thousands of relationships. However, I still have my gracious and merciful Lord, my beautiful wife Cameron, my children and grandchildren, real friends, and a church family that loves unconditionally.

I want to encourage you by telling you from my own experience that failure, pain, rejection, and even consequences all have an expiration date. Even if it was by your own hand, what you have endured is God's preparation ground for a beautiful new life that will be more authentic. I have never been more qualified to be a genuine minister and a loyal friend than I am today. You will make it out of the darkness. What the enemy meant for your destruction; God will turn into your divine destiny. You will fulfill your God-given potential. Cindy Trimm says, "Potential, simply put, is dormant ability, reserved power, untapped strength, unused success, hidden talents, and capped capability." You are a threat to the enemy. That is why he has fought you so hard. Your God-given potential has been locked up in illegitimate relationships. Now that you've lost, you've actually won. The only way you fail is to quit Again, I quote Cindy Trimm: "Refuse to let your history interfere with your destiny!" Have a funeral for your past, take control of your thoughts, get a divine download of who you are today and speak it over yourself every day![1]

2

The High Cost of Betrayal

David Betrayed by His Own Heart

The question is not what was different about Bathsheba. The difference was what had become different about David.

Johnny Hunt[2]

In the spring, at the time when kings go off to war, David sent Joab out with the king's men and the whole Israelite army. They destroyed the Ammonites and besieged Rabbah. But David remained in Jerusalem.

One evening David got up from his bed and walked around on the roof of the palace. From the roof he saw a woman bathing. The woman was very beautiful, and David sent someone to find out about her. The man said, "She is Bathsheba, the daughter of Eliam and the wife of Uriah the Hittite."

Then David sent messengers to get her. She came to him, and he slept with her. (Now she was purifying

---

[2] http://www.morefamousquotes.com/quotes/3649842-the-question-is-not-what-was-different.html accessed March 2, 2021.

> *herself from her monthly uncleanness.) Then she went back home.*
>
> *The woman conceived and sent word to David, saying, "I am pregnant."*
>
> 2 Samuel 11:1-5

I love the Bible because it never covers up the sins of God's people. The Bible presents the facts, draws out the lessons, and leaves truly little for us to speculate about its meaning.

Such was the case with David and Bathsheba. The sordid tale is all out there—in plain English—for the entire world to see.

I doubt when David did what he did that he would have ever imagined that movies would be made, and books would be written about him thousands of years after the fact. David is a reminder that Numbers 32:23 is real, "But if you fail to do this, you will be sinning against the Lord; and you may be sure that your sin will find you out."

The Bible tells us that David was the son of Jesse and the great-grandson of Ruth and Boaz. He was a brilliant musician, a writer of some of the most beloved Psalms. The only person in the Bible that God declared was "a man after mine own heart."

> *After removing Saul, he made David their king. God testified concerning him: 'I have found David son of Jesse, a man after my own heart; he will do everything I want him to do.'*
>
> Acts 13:22

Yet, with his solid heritage, humble beginnings, and a heart devoted to the Lord, David was guilty of adultery, lying, and conspiracy to commit murder. Before you condemn David for his sin, it would be wise to remember that most, if not all, of us, have walked where David walked. David is a perfect example of how there are times when God's people can do things that would seem to contradict the very God who lives inside of them. Looking at David and saying, "I would never do that" is a familiar refrain. But the fact remains we are all subject to the lusts of the flesh when left unguarded by the power of the Holy Spirit. Jeremiah 17:9 (NLT) declares, "The human heart is the most deceitful of all things, and desperately wicked. Who really knows how bad it is?"

The Bible records this about David:

> *For David had done what was right in the eyes of the Lord and had not failed to keep any of the Lord's commands all the days of his life—except in the case of Uriah the Hittite.*
>
> 1 Kings 15:5

God declared that David obeyed all His commandments and did what was right all the days of his life but there is that nagging except thrown in at the end of the statement.

Did you catch the phrase at the end? "Except in the case of Uriah the Hittite." It's great news for God to brag on you, but He had to throw the exception in there. I am afraid if God talked to somebody about me, there would probably be more excepts than there would be great complements.

David lived on a virtual spiritual roller coaster. David could be rejoicing over victories one day, and the next day he would be languishing in the deepest valley of depression (read Psalms 42-43). I am convinced that God never intended us to live a roller coaster life—up one day and down the next.

David knew the pain of betrayal by his covenant friend, Jonathan. David would soon feel the sharp cut of betrayal when his son Absalom would attempt to depose him from the throne. But David is about to feel a different type of betrayal—one he had never felt before—from his own heart!

Let's examine how far this man would go to have his way and what the consequences of his actions would produce.

Consider David's Sin

All of us know the story. There is nothing new here. But I find it's helpful and practical to go back and refresh our thinking with some of the more familiar stories in the Bible.

David's sin is one of those episodes.

David was no ordinary guy hanging out looking for a good time. No. He was the king, and he was clothed with immense power. David was probably a middle-aged man by now and should have known better than to act like some wild-eyed teenager.

How does a man like David, a man "after God's own heart," end up in so much self-deception? David had everything that his heart desired—wealth, power, and unquestioned loyalty from his subjects. Yet here we are talking about a man who had everything and was willing to let it all go to feed his lustful desires.

It's not hard to see how David walked into this sin.

He was over-confident. After years of struggle, David was finally able to realize God's promise. He was no longer a shepherd boy or a teenage giant killer; he is now the anointed king. David is in the palace enjoying victories and prosperity. It would certainly appear that all was well in the kingdom. Sadly, the story doesn't end with David enjoying the fruits of his victories. David was too important in his own eyes, and it will cost him dearly.

Disobedient

> *In the spring, at the time when kings go off to war, David sent Joab out with the king's men and the whole Israelite army. They destroyed the Ammonites and besieged Rabbah. But David remained in Jerusalem.*
>
> 2 Samuel 11:1

For some reason, David decided to stay at the palace when he should have been leading his men into battle. We have no idea why David decided that it was time for him to relinquish his role of leading his army into battle to Joab, but he did. We can see the contrast between David's faithful men, who were willing to sacrifice their lives, and David, who stayed at home—out of danger.

Self-Indulgent

One evening David got up from his bed and walked around on the roof of the palace. From the roof he saw a woman bathing. The woman was very beautiful, and David sent someone to find out about her. The man said, "She is Bathsheba, the daughter of Eliam and the wife of Uriah the Hittite." Then David sent messengers to get her. She came to him, and he slept with her. (Now she was purifying herself from her monthly uncleanness.) Then she went back home. The woman conceived and sent word to David, saying, "I am pregnant."

2 Samuel 11:2-5

If you want to know what privilege looks like, examine how David reacts when he sees a beautiful woman. Instead of disciplining himself, he gives in to his desires and becomes careless. He allowed his eyes to wander and yielded to the "lust of the flesh" and the "lust of the eyes" (See 1 John 2:16).

James 1:13-15 gives us a New Testament description of just how David's sin unfolded.

When tempted, no one should say, "God is tempting me." For God cannot be tempted by evil, nor does he tempt anyone; but each person is tempted when they are dragged away by their own evil desire and enticed. Then, after desire has conceived, it gives birth to sin; and sin, when it is full-grown, gives birth to death.

- David's desires were activated by the sight of Bathsheba, and he did not turn away.
- David's desire birthed sin in his mind.
- David gave in to his desire, and this led to his sin.
- David's sin led to death.

It is not a sin to be tempted. David could have avoided this disaster if he had recalled the clear command given in Exodus 20:14, "You shall not commit adultery," or the fact that Bathsheba was a man's daughter and a man's wife.

Did you know that the Bible tells us that Bathsheba was married to one of David's bravest soldiers? (2 Samuel 23:39). And was also the granddaughter of Ahithophel, who later sided with Absalom in his rebellion against David? (2 Samuel 23:34; chapters 16-17).

I know that it takes two to cooperate, but David bears the most significant responsibility for this sin. After all, he was the king and could have had more wives if he had wanted them. All he had to do, according to 2 Samuel 12:8, was ask. Instead of telling the Lord he was unhappy with what he had, David decided to take something that didn't belong to him.

Sin Led to His Cover-Up

James 1:15 warns us, "Then, after desire has conceived, it gives birth to sin; and sin, when it is full-grown, gives birth to death." How fitting are those words in the case of David's sin?

A Master Manipulator

He tried to manipulate Uriah. Instead of confessing his sin and asking for forgiveness, David does the unthinkable. He sent for Bathsheba's husband and tried to trick him into going home. Had Uriah complied with the king's request to sleep with his wife, David's dilemma would have been solved, or so he thought.

> *So David sent this word to Joab: "Send me Uriah the Hittite." And Joab sent him to David. When Uriah came to him, David asked him how Joab was, how the soldiers were and how the war was going. Then David said to Uriah, "Go down to your house and wash your feet." So Uriah left the palace, and a gift from the king was sent after him. But Uriah slept at the entrance to the palace with all his master's servants and did not go down to his house.*
>
> 2 Samuel 11:6-9

Uriah was a better man, and it showed when he refused the king's request to go home and be with his wife. It's easy to compare David's self-indulgence and disobedience with Uriah's self-discipline.

> *Uriah said to David, "The ark and Israel and Judah are staying in tents, and my commander Joab and my lord's men are camped in the open country. How could I go to my house to eat and drink and make love to my wife? As surely as you live, I will not do such a thing!*
>
> 2 Samuel 11:11

David tried one last attempt to trick Uriah by making him drunk. But even a drunk Uriah was a more noble and disciplined man than a sober David.

> *Then David said to him, "Stay here one more day, and tomorrow I will send you back." So Uriah remained in Jerusalem that day and the next. At David's invitation, he ate and drank with him, and David made him drunk. But in the evening Uriah went out to sleep on his mat among his master's servants; he did not go home.*
>
> 2 Samuel 11:12-13

He tried to manipulate Joab. The plot thickens, and sin continues to grow. David included his army commander in his cover-up. The plan was simple: Uriah had to die. And the best way for him to be removed was to die in battle. It would be a glorious death, and no one would be the wiser.

Joab was more than willing to co-operate since this would give him leverage to take advantage of David. It's sad to think, but Uriah carried his death warrant to the battlefield that day.

> *In the morning David wrote a letter to Joab and sent it with Uriah. In it he wrote, "Put Uriah out in front where the fighting is fiercest. Then withdraw from him so he will be struck down and die." So while Joab had the city under siege, he put Uriah at a place where he knew the strongest defenders were. When the men of the city came out and fought against Joab, some of the men in David's army fell; moreover, Uriah the Hittite died.*
>
> 2 Samuel 11:14-17

The plan worked. The deed was done. A brave soldier died that day. And all that was left was for David to put on a show during the week of mourning. No doubt there were some in the palace that probably remarked how thoughtful it was for the king to comfort the widow of Uriah. Little did they know that it was the king who orchestrated the horrible affair, and soon the widow would be the king's wife.

> *When Uriah's wife heard that her husband was dead, she mourned for him. After the time of mourning was over, David had her brought to his house, and she became his wife and bore him a son. But the thing David had done displeased the Lord.*
>
> 2 Samuel 11:26

He tried to manipulate the Lord. David may have fooled others. He may have thought the cover-up worked, but he is about to find out the truth of Proverbs 28:13 which says, "Whoever conceals their sins does not prosper, but the one who confesses and renounces them finds mercy."

A cover-up never works. David thought only three people knew what went on—himself, Bathsheba, and Joab.

But David didn't reckon on the fact that the Lord knew. And that's all that mattered. "But the thing David had done displeased the Lord."

Cleansing

At least a year passed since David committed the sins of adultery and murder. He was sure the cover-up was solid, and no one would ever find out what he had done. But 2 Samuel 11:27 ended with that solemn phrase, "But the thing David had done displeased the Lord." David thought no one knew, but he forgot that God knows all things.

Before David is forgiven, he undergoes a painful process that could have been avoided.

Confession

If you want to know what David's life has been like during the days of keeping the cover-up from unraveling, read Psalms 32 and 51.

When I kept silent,
my bones wasted away
through my groaning all day long.
For day and night
your hand was heavy on me;
my strength was sapped
as in the heat of summer.

Psalm 32:3-4

Let me hear joy and gladness;
let the bones you have crushed rejoice.
Hide your face from my sins
and blot out all my iniquity.

Betrayal

> *Create in me a pure heart, O God,*
> *and renew a steadfast spirit within me.*
> *Do not cast me from your presence*
> *or take your Holy Spirit from me.*
> *Restore to me the joy of your salvation*
> *and grant me a willing spirit, to sustain me.*
> *Then I will teach transgressors your ways,*
> *so that sinners will turn back to you.*
>
> Psalm 51:8-13

- He was weak and sick physically.
- He lost his joy.
- He lost his witness for the Lord.
- He lost his anointing.
- He lost the ability to hear God's voice.
- He lost his spiritual vision.

God gave David plenty of time to come clean. But David persisted in hiding his sin. I am convinced had David repented sooner rather than later, the consequences of his sin would not have been as severe.

The Lord revealed David's sin to his pastor, the faithful prophet, by the name of Nathan. 2 Samuel 12 shows that Nathan did not come to bring a blessing but a message of conviction. No doubt it took a lot of courage for Nathan to stand in the presence of the king and declare, "Thou art the man!"

> *Then Nathan said to David, "You are the man! This is what the Lord, the God of Israel, says: 'I anointed you king over Israel, and I delivered you from the hand of Saul. I gave your master's house to you, and your master's wives into your arms. I gave you all Israel and Judah. And if all this had been too little, I would have given you even more. Why did you despise the word of the Lord by doing what is evil in his eyes? You*

struck down Uriah the Hittite with the sword and took his wife to be your own. You killed him with the sword of the Ammonites. Now, therefore, the sword will never depart from your house, because you despised me and took the wife of Uriah the Hittite to be your own.'
"This is what the Lord says: 'Out of your own household I am going to bring calamity on you. Before your very eyes I will take your wives and give them to one who is close to you, and he will sleep with your wives in broad daylight. You did it in secret, but I will do this thing in broad daylight before all Israel.'"

Then David said to Nathan, "I have sinned against the Lord."

Nathan replied, "The Lord has taken away your sin. You are not going to die. But because by doing this you have shown utter contempt for the Lord, the son born to you will die."

2 Samuel 12:7-14

Chastisement

David surrendered to the word of the Lord and admitted his sin. Then David said to Nathan, "I have sinned against the Lord." God was ready to forgive David, but in God's government, He could not prevent those sins from bringing forth death, (see James 1:15).

Nathan declared to David in 2 Samuel 12:10, "Now, therefore, the sword will never depart from your house."

There would be a four-fold payment for David's sin.

1. His secret sin would become public (2 Samuel 12:12)
2. The baby died (2 Samuel 12:15-18)
3. Absalom killed Amon, who raped Tamar (2 Samuel 13)
4. Joab killed Absalom (2 Samuel 18:9-17)

Sadly, David would spend the next few years paying for his momentary act of lustful pleasure. Think about it for a moment. The scripture is clear—a man will reap what he sows (see Galatians 6:7), and David is proof that scripture is real. Every evil thing that David sowed came back to him many times over. He sowed lust and reaped the same; he sowed murder and reaped murder, etc.

The good news is what started as a sordid affair ended up with David back on the battlefield leading his army to victory (see 2 Samuel 12:26-31). David confessed his sins; God forgave him; now he could—with the complete confidence of the Lord—fight for his nation again. David and Bathsheba's story is a traumatic one, but also one that God redeems. It stands as a clear warning to every leader, every spouse, and every believer who loves God and feels secure in their perspectives. The story reveals the consequences of feeding secret lustful desires. Even a heart like David's can be deceitful and wicked. The heart can fool any of us and destroy the best of us (see Jeremiah 17:9). We must all be actively aware of the battle for our hearts (see 1 Peter 5:8-10) and respond accordingly, with the power of the Holy Spirit (see Ephesians 6:10-18).[3]

A Final Thought

Please remember that one of Satan's most effective weapons is to accuse us when we fail the Lord (see Revelation 12:7-12). Oh, how the enemy loves to stand before God and point out our sins and shortcomings (see Job 1).

David had plenty of issues, and yes, David committed horrible sins. But God did not condemn him to a life of misery and failure. God did not judge David's entire life based on his sin with Bathsheba. His sin did not cancel out all the wonderful things he did—not by a long shot!

---

[3] https://www.crosswalk.com/faith/bible-study/things-to-know-about-david-and-bathsheba.html accessed April 2, 2021.

Once David was willing to confess his sin, God was more than willing to forgive and restore him (see Psalms 37, 51). If God had written David off, you would not have read what God thought about him:

> *I have found David son of Jesse, a man after my own heart;*
> *he will do everything I want him to do*
>
> Acts 13:22

I have discovered that you don't have to do what David did to learn the lessons that David learned.

- But when we do fall short—it's not over.
- When we fail, God is ready and willing to forgive.
- God is not looking for perfect people—there aren't any.
- Our sin does not cancel out all the good things we have accomplished.
- Satan is a liar; God will use us despite our shortcomings.

3

Beware the Absalom Spirit!

Betrayed by family

It's a shame that the very people who you protect are the first ones to turn their backs on you.

Autumn Kohler

In all Israel there was not a man so highly praised for his handsome appearance as Absalom. From the top of his head to the sole of his foot there was no blemish in him. Whenever he cut the hair of his head—he used to cut his hair once a year because it became too heavy for him—he would weigh it, and its weight was two hundred shekels by the royal standard.

2 Samuel 14:25-26

There is probably no hurt more devastating than the damage caused by the betrayal of our flesh and blood. When friends betray us, we can always ask God to bring new friends into our lives. But when blood betrays us, there is no assuaging the devastation one might feel.

One overriding fact about Absalom's sad story applies to all of us; at some point, people will disappoint and betray us. It's a fact of life that most of us don't want to admit. Why? Because we don't want to consider that people—including family members—would ever turn their backs on us. As seen in the life of Absalom, people are not perfect. If we stay in a relationship long enough, including marriage and ministry, we WILL experience the tragedy of betrayal.

History is filled with examples of betrayal, and none more famous than Marcus Brutus.

> No treachery is worse than betrayal by a family member or friend. Julius Caesar knew such treachery. Among the conspirators who assassinated the Roman leader on March 15, 44 B. C. was Marcus Junius Brutus. Caesar not only trusted Brutus, he had favored him as a son. According to Roman historians, Caesar first resisted the onslaught of the assassins. But when he saw Brutus among them with his dagger drawn, Caesar ceased to struggle and, pulling the top part of his robe over his face, asked the famous question, "You too, Brutus?"[4]

Marcus Brutus was not the first to commit an act of betrayal, and you can rest assured he is not the last.

In this chapter, we will examine one of the most heinous acts of betrayal ever committed. I want us to examine the character, characteristics, the culmination of the Absalom spirit, and the spirit of betrayal.

Absalom Spirit

When looking into the character of an Absalom spirit, you first have to consider the natural.

The story of Absalom is outlined in 2 Samuel chapters 13-18. It is clear from scripture that Absalom was a real person who demonstrated many wonderful attributes. Unfortunately, some of his most admired

---

[4] *Today in the Word*, August 13, 1992. https://www.family-times.net/illustration/Betrayal/200922/ accessed February 1, 2021.

characteristics would turn out to be his downfall. His strengths would eventually become his weakness and lead to his destruction.

As the son of King David, Absalom had a lot of things going for him. He was so handsome that one might say if he were alive today, he would be a fashion model. He was a physical specimen unrivaled in all the kingdom.

> *In all Israel there was not a man so highly praised for his handsome appearance as Absalom. From the top of his head to the sole of his foot there was no blemish in him.*
>
> 2 Samuel 14:25

It appears from reading the scripture that Absalom was not content with his standing as a son of the king. He displayed an attitude of spiritual pride and was easily offended. His frustration led him down a dark path that would eventually create chaos, confusion, and death. People who possess the Absalom spirit are typically frustrated with their lives, their ministries, or their perceived level in life. They often search for value in personal pursuits rather than in God Himself and thus become like the man Solomon described:

> *Throughout their lives, they live under a cloud—frustrated, discouraged, and angry*
>
> Ecclesiastes 5:17 (NLT)[5]

The second aspect of the character of Absalom is spiritual. The spirit of Absalom is alive and operating today and is no respecter of persons. The modern church landscape attests to the fact that this spirit has caused irreparable damage to the Gospel of Christ. Much like the name Judas, or Jezebel, the mention of Absalom evokes disobedience, pride, self-aggrandizement, hypocrisy, and rebellion. If we are not

---

[5] https://davewilliams.com/dealing-with-the-absalom-spirit/ accessed February 1, 2021.

vigilant, the spirit of Absalom will spread the poison of betrayal and leave a trail of destruction in its wake.

In his book *Love Like You've Never Been Hurt*, Jentezen Franklin recounts the assassination of the twentieth President of the United States, James Garfield.

> James Garfield had only been president of the United States for four months when he was shot in the back on July 2, 1881, by a would-be assassin. He lived just three months more.
>
> You would think it was the shot that killed him. It wasn't.
>
> You see, the bullet did not penetrate any vital organs. It got stuck behind his pancreas, but it was not a fatal injury. But back then, doctors weren't concerned about germs; they did not even believe they existed because they couldn't see them. So, minutes after President Garfield was shot, doctors pressed in around him to stick their fingers and push unsterilized instruments into his wound. They poked and prodded as far as they could in his body, hoping to find the bullet and remove it. They continued to do this for eighty days while President Garfield languished in the hospital. As we today would expect, this regular unsterilized digging worsened the president's condition. He developed infections and eventually died.
>
> I find it fascinating that President Garfield did not succumb to death because of the bullet wound. He died from the infections caused by the doctors who kept probing the wound.[6]

What happened to President Garfield—in the natural—resulted from not recognizing the seriousness of how germs can spread. As in

---

[6] Jentezen Franklin, *Love Like You've Never Been Hurt*, (Minneapolis, MN: Chosen Publishing Group, 2018) 14-15.

the case of Garfield, without proper care, the infection will eventually lead to death.

The spirit of Absalom, when unchecked, can spread a spiritual infection through the body of Christ. My friend, we must take all precautions never to allow this insidious spirit to gain a foothold in our families, businesses, or our churches.

When we look into the first major event in Absalom's life that caused him deep hurt, we go to 2 Samuel 13. When Absalom found out that his sister, Tamar, was raped by their half-brother Amnon, he was beside himself with rage, vowing to take revenge. Absalom insisted that Tamar live with him, and he fully expected his father, David, to come and do something about the situation. David didn't come. For two years, the poison of hate coursed through his veins against his father, David, and Amnon.

> *Now Absalom had commanded his servants, saying, "Watch now, when Amnon's heart is merry with wine, and when I say to you, 'Strike Amnon!' then kill him. Do not be afraid. Have I not commanded you? Be courageous and valiant." So the servants of Absalom did to Amnon as Absalom had commanded. Then all the king's sons arose, and each one got on his mule and fled. And it came to pass, while they were on the way, that news came to David, saying, "Absalom has killed all the king's sons, and not one of them is left!" So the king arose and tore his garments and lay on the ground, and all his servants stood by with their clothes torn. Then Jonadab the son of Shimeah, David's brother, answered and said, "Let not my lord suppose they have killed all the young men, the king's sons, for only Amnon is dead. For by the command of Absalom this has been determined from the day that he forced his sister Tamar. Now therefore, let not my lord the*

> *king take the thing to his heart, to think that all the king's sons are dead. For only Amnon is dead."*
>
> 2 Samuel 13:28-33 (NKJV)

Let's be clear, according to the culture and law, Absalom had every legal right to avenge his sister, Tamar. However, holding a grudge, refusing to forgive, and taking vengeance into one's own hands only brings destruction and death to the heart of the one refusing to reconcile.

Let's examine the characteristics of an Absalom spirit. Holding grudges and refusing to forgive others. This is the beginning of deception in Absalom; it always starts with refusing to forgive others.

Rejoicing in vengeance and refusing to extend grace. This is another aspect of an Absalom spirit, and it comes out of this same tragic event. The adage "two wrongs don't make a right," was never truer than in this situation. Just because you have a right to retaliate, doesn't make it right if you do.

We move from this tragic event to another characteristic of an Absalom spirit. An Absalom spirit throws temper tantrums to get its way.

> *And Absalom dwelt two full years in Jerusalem, but did not see the king's face. Therefore Absalom sent for Joab, to send him to the king, but he would not come to him. And when he sent again the second time, he would not come. So he said to his servants, "See, Joab's field is near mine, and he has barley there; go and set it on fire." And Absalom's servants set the field on fire. Then Joab arose and came to Absalom's house, and said to him, "Why have your servants set my field on fire?" And Absalom answered Joab, "Look, I sent to you, saying, 'Come here, so that I may send you to the king, to say, "Why have I come from Geshur? It would be better for me to be there still."*

> *'Now therefore, let me see the king's face; but if there is iniquity in me, let him execute me." So Joab went to the king and told him. And when he had called for Absalom, he came to the king and bowed himself on his face to the ground before the king. Then the king kissed Absalom.*
>
> 2 Samuel 14:28-33 (NKJV)

Absalom is a spoiled rotten brat! Can you imagine burning down another man's field full of crops just to force him to create a meeting between you and your father? This is rage out of control.

Absalom began an undercover operation to take the throne from his father with vengeance on his mind and hate in his heart. It was so subtle that Absalom almost pulled it off. In this attempted coup d'état, we see two more characteristics of an Absalom spirit.

The Absalom spirit never works alone. It/he must have an entourage. 2 Samuel 15:1 says, "Absalom provided himself with chariots and horses and fifty men." As if to say, "Don't you know who I am, and how important I am?" This looks and sounds a lot like the western church and the big shot preachers that carry their entourage with them everywhere they go.

An Absalom spirit manipulates people. How? By magnifying the mistakes of others to gain influence and loyalty with the people they want to win over.

> *In the course of time, Absalom provided himself with a chariot and horses and with fifty men to run ahead of him. He would get up early and stand by the side of the road leading to the city gate. Whenever anyone came with a complaint to be placed before the king for a decision, Absalom would call out to him, "What town are you from?" He would answer, "Your servant is from one of the tribes of Israel." Then Absalom would say to him, "Look, your claims are valid and*

> *proper, but there is no representative of the king to hear you." And Absalom would add, "If only I were appointed judge in the land! Then everyone who has a complaint or case could come to me and I would see that they receive justice."*
>
> *Also, whenever anyone approached him to bow down before him, Absalom would reach out his hand, take hold of him and kiss him. Absalom behaved in this way toward all the Israelites who came to the king asking for justice, and so he stole the hearts of the people of Israel.*
>
> 2 Samuel 15:1-6

After about four years, "Absalom stole the hearts of the men of Israel." His campaign of undermining the king, his own father, was successful and David had to leave the throne.

Pastor Mark Driscoll observed:

An unhealed father wound that invites the Absalom spirit compels men (and sometimes women) to believe that if they were in the position of highest leadership, they would do a better job of defending the hurting and caring for the needy. As a result, they seek to form unholy alliances and overthrow established governance. This can be a son overtaking a father in the home, a spiritual son overtaking a spiritual father in a church, or a team member overtaking a leader in an organization. Though evil and proud, it is done in the name of love, care, and protection, much like Satan, who felt he could do a better job than God and had angels who felt the same.[7]

---

[7] https://realfaith.com/daily-devotions/the-absalom-spirit/ accessed February 3, 2021.

In the end, Absalom was so full of poison that he led the charge to kill his father and eliminate any opposition. His goal was to ascend to the throne.

Another characteristic of an Absalom spirit is that it/he surrounds himself with your enemies. 2 Samuel 15:12 (NKJV)

> *Then Absalom sent for Ahithophel the Gilonite, David's counselor, from his city—from Giloh—while he offered sacrifices and the conspiracy grew strong, for the people with Absalom continually increased in number.*
>
> 2 Samuel 15:12 (NKJV)

Ahithophel just happened to be Bathsheba's grandfather and it is believed that he hated David for what he did to his family.

An Absalom spirit also has a characteristic of loving to get people to agree with them about how right they are and how bad you are. In 2 Samuel 15 this was his tactic, to get the people to see David's flaws and turn to him—Absalom—as their answer. Ultimately these tactics and conspiracies produce the characteristic in someone who becomes your competition and is incapable of complimenting you.

Another characteristic of an Absalom spirit is removing those who disagree with them. In 2 Samuel 17, Absalom didn't like Ahithophel's counsel, so he removed him for Hushai. Why did he do that? Because Hushai told him what he wanted to hear. It also ended up getting him killed.

In over 35 years of ministry, I have personally witnessed leaders who cannot and will not tolerate being corrected or challenged. I'm not talking about insubordination; I'm talking about someone who loves you enough to tell you the truth. In fact, I even heard one ministry leader say, "There is no man qualified for me to answer to or to hold me accountable." I suggest if you find yourself under that kind of delusionary leader you should run and run fast.

Betrayal

The most overriding characteristic of an Absalom spirit is that they are driven by self-recognition and power that are the result of their own insecurities.

> *Now Absalom happened to meet David's men. He was riding his mule, and as the mule went under the thick branches of a large oak, Absalom's hair got caught in the tree. He was left hanging in midair, while the mule he was riding kept on going.*
>
> *When one of the men saw what had happened, he told Joab, "I just saw Absalom hanging in an oak tree."*
>
> *Joab said to the man who had told him this, "What! You saw him? Why didn't you strike him to the ground right there? Then I would have had to give you ten shekels of silver and a warrior's belt."*
>
> *But the man replied, "Even if a thousand shekels were weighed out into my hands, I would not lay a hand on the king's son. In our hearing the king commanded you and Abishai and Ittai, 'Protect the young man Absalom for my sake' And if I had put my life in jeopardy—and nothing is hidden from the king—you would have kept your distance from me."*
>
> *Joab said, "I'm not going to wait like this for you." So he took three javelins in his hand and plunged them into Absalom's heart while Absalom was still alive in the oak tree. And ten of Joab's armor-bearers surrounded Absalom, struck him and killed him.*
>
> 2 Samuel 18:9-15

Absalom's hair was his glory and his identity. He gets hung by his glory and his identity and it becomes his complete demise. I have learned that any person who uses their position, influence, wealth, or success to manipulate you is a person who has no self-worth and is insecure. Thus, we have this type of leadership in the church today. Most people in ministry are the most insecure people I've ever met. Therefore, they constantly bob and weave, counter, and manipulate to keep anyone from finding out just how insecure they are.

Remember, any person who uses their position, influence, wealth, success, or relationship to manipulate you is a person who has no self-worth. I have found that most Type A personalities are the most insecure people in the world.

We've looked at the character and the characteristics of an Absalom spirit, now let's watch the culmination of being an Absalom.

What Is The End Of An Absalom?

A sad fact is a betrayer will be left with no legacy!

> *Now Absalom in his lifetime had taken and set up a pillar for himself, which is in the King's Valley. For he said, 'I have no son to keep my name in remembrance.' He called the pillar after his own name. And to this day it is called Absalom's Monument.*
>
> 2 Samuel 18:18 (NKJV)

Is that true? Did Absalom have no son?

No, he had three sons.

2 Samuel 14:27 tells us something different, "To Absalom were born three sons, and one daughter whose name was Tamar. She was a woman of beautiful appearance."

Here's the tragedy: It was not that Absalom had no sons. It was that he had no sons who would remember his name. So, he had to build his own legacy. A modern-day Absalom is not interested in leaving a legacy for his children, but a legacy that is a monument unto himself.

Absalom's rebellion came to a tragic end just like so many others who thought they could usurp God's anointed. Names like Jezebel,

Betrayal

Korah, Dathan, Abiram, and Judas. Their downfall was pride, and as a result, their lives ended prematurely and tragically.

Warning: The Lord does not take kindly to those who sow strife and discord among the body of Christ. The modern-day Absaloms may think that their rebellion will gain the preeminence they crave. But reread the account of Absalom and see the results of his pride.

> *Pride goes before destruction, a haughty spirit before a fall. Better to be lowly in spirit along with the oppressed than to share plunder with the proud.*
>
> Proverbs 16:18-19
>
> *Consequently, whoever rebels against the authority is rebelling against what God has instituted, and those who do so will bring judgment on themselves.*
>
> Romans 13:2

A nation can survive its fools, and even the ambitious. But it cannot survive treason from within. An enemy at the gates is less formidable, for he is known and carries his banner openly. But the traitor moves amongst those within the gate freely, his sly whispers rustling through all the alleys, heard in the very halls of government itself. For the traitor appears not a traitor; he speaks in accents familiar to his victims, and he wears their face and their arguments, he appeals to the baseness that lies deep in the hearts of all men. He rots the soul of a nation, he works secretly and unknown in the night to undermine the pillars of the city, he infects the body politic so that it can no longer resist. A murderer is less to be feared.

Marcus Tullius Cicero 42 B.C. [8]

---

[8] Cicero's speech to the Roman Senate, as recorded by Sallust, quoted in Taylor Caldwell, *A Pillar of Iron: A Novel About Cicero and the Rome He*

A Final Thought

How did David handle Absalom's betrayal? It is never easy to think about or deal with a family member's betrayal. David was willing to allow God to have control over the situation. When David heard the news that Absalom had been killed, he didn't rejoice—he wept. Yes, David won the victory and would assume the duties of King, but there was no rejoicing over losing a son that he loved.

> *The king was shaken. He went up to the room over the gateway and wept. As he went, he said: 'O my son Absalom! My son, my son Absalom! If only I had died instead of you—O Absalom, my son, my son!'*
>
> 2 Samuel 18:33

Tried to Save, (New York: Doubleday & Company, Inc., 1965), p.556. https://forums.anandtech.com/threads/this-is-a-popular-quote-people-like-to-throw-around-but-find-me-where-it-is-from.234376/ accessed February 1, 2021.

4

How Did I End Up Here?

Joseph Betrayed by His Brothers

Joseph did not endure the pit, Potiphar's House, and prison because he knew he would end up in the Pharaoh's Palace. He simply remained faithful wherever he found himself. God did the rest.

H.B. Charles, Jr.

Joseph said to them, "Do not be afraid, for am I in the place of God? But as for you, you meant evil against me; but God meant it for good, in order to bring it about as it is this day, to save many people alive. Now therefore, do not be afraid; I will provide for you and your little ones." And he comforted them and spoke kindly to them.

Genesis 50:19-21

In 2011, Kelly Clarkson released a song entitled: Stronger (What Doesn't Kill You). This song could have been a theme for the life of Joseph. It could also be said that even after all of the challenges he faced that Joseph's life ends up well. He had quite the journey getting to the place where he was the second most powerful man in the most powerful nation in the known world.

At age 30, we see him standing before Pharaoh. In Genesis, we read.

> *So Pharaoh asked them, "Can we find anyone like this man, one in whom is the spirit of God?" Then Pharaoh said to Joseph, "Since God has made all this known to you, there is no one so discerning and wise as you. You shall be in charge of my palace, and all my people are to submit to your orders. Only with respect to the throne will I be greater than you." So Pharaoh said to Joseph, "I hereby put you in charge of the whole land of Egypt." Then Pharaoh took his signet ring from his finger and put it on Joseph's finger. He dressed him in robes of fine linen and put a gold chain around his neck. [43] He had him ride in a chariot as his second-in-command, and people shouted before him, "Make way!" Thus he put him in charge of the whole land of Egypt.*
>
> Genesis 41:38-43

A little later, Joseph makes the statement to his brothers.

> *So now it was not you who sent me here, but God; and He has made me a father to Pharaoh, and lord of all his house, and a ruler throughout all the land of Egypt.*
>
> Genesis 45:8 (NKJV)

Reading what Pharaoh said about Joseph and how the end was far greater than the beginning, it would be easy to overlook all the pain and suffering it took for Joseph to end up in such a powerful position.

Joseph followed and maintained a strict protocol regardless of his circumstances or surroundings that led to promotion. That's why I believe Joseph's life was elevated out of a pit of slavery, established in

Potiphar's house after being falsely accused of rape by Potiphar's wife, equipped in prison interpreting dreams, and exalted to the second most powerful man in the world by Pharaoh.

Before we get to Joseph's strict protocol, we need to establish a little background.

Joseph was the firstborn of Rachael, his father Jacob's favorite wife. His father named him prophetically because his name means, "let him add" or increaser.

> *Now Israel loved Joseph more than all his children, because he was the son of his old age. Also he made him a tunic of many colors.*
>
> Genesis 37:3 (NKJV)

In the life of Joseph, we see one of the few people in the Bible about whom nothing evil is reported. He was born with Adam's nature, just as we are, but there isn't any known sin recorded with his name attached. No known sin, in itself, leads us to view Joseph as an Old Testament type of Christ.

There are many misinterpretations of his tunic. Translated, it was a tunic of many lengths, which in that culture represented that Joseph would be the primary heir of Israel. He would receive the double portion of the inheritance rather than Rueben, the oldest son. Why? It's not a mystery—Jacob told us at the end of his life.

> *Reuben, you are my firstborn, my might and the beginning of my strength, The excellency of dignity and the excellency of power. Unstable as water, you shall not excel, because you went up to your father's bed; then you defiled it—he went up to my couch.*
>
> Genesis 49:3-4 (NKJV)

This translation from Hebrew is rather gracious. Literally in Hebrew, he called him a leprous scab and said he was full of puss boiling over with lust. Rueben slept with Jacob's concubine Bilhah, who was Rachael's handmaid. It's interesting that Bilhah means, "fear" and comes from a root word in Hebrew that means, "in a hurry." So, I think it's safe to say, based on Rueben's experience, that anytime you listen to your flesh, get in a hurry and go to bed with fear, you lose your legacy and harvest!

An Incredible Journey

Let's follow Joseph's incredible journey that took him from the pit of despair to the Pharaoh's throne.

Joseph had a prophetic dream. Every dream carries the seeds of a promised future. A dream becomes the North Star of your life that shines even in difficulty. We all need a guide post that gives direction and purpose to our ever-changing circumstances. In the immortal words of that great philosopher Yogi Berra, "If you don't know where you're going, you could wind up someplace else!"

God gave Joseph two dreams, and they would come to pass—but as the drama unfolds, we see that it didn't sit well with his brothers.

> *Now Joseph had a dream, and he told it to his brothers; and they hated him even more. So he said to them, "Please hear this dream which I have dreamed: There we were, binding sheaves in the field. Then behold, my sheaf arose and also stood upright; and indeed your sheaves stood all around and bowed down to my sheaf."*
>
> *And his brothers said to him, "Shall you indeed reign over us? Or shall you indeed have dominion over us?" So they hated him even more for his dreams and for his words.*
>
> *Then he dreamed still another dream and told it to his brothers, and said, "Look, I have dreamed another*

dream. And this time, the sun, the moon, and the eleven stars bowed down to me."

So he told it to his father and his brothers; and his father rebuked him and said to him, "What is this dream that you have dreamed? Shall your mother and I and your brothers indeed come to bow down to the earth before you?" And his brothers envied him, but his father kept the matter in mind.

Genesis 37:5-11 (NKJV)

The first Christian martyr, Stephen, told us in Acts 7:9 (NKJV) that Joseph's brothers were moved with envy, or as the Greek has it, jealousy. "And the patriarchs, becoming envious, sold Joseph into Egypt. But God was with him."

The dreams given to him by God were symbols of future power, and they were so clear as to exert a tremendous effect upon his character. Joseph was a man with a goal, and he moved steadily toward it. It became apparent that Joseph's brothers were so consumed by jealousy that they would do whatever it took to rob him of his destiny. They did not want him to have what they could not have and what they could not become.

> Some think that Joseph made a mistake in telling the dream to his brethren. But he seemed to be motivated not by self-esteem or vanity but by the naiveté of youth. Some may think that telling the dream brought disaster, but "God moves in mysterious ways, His wonders to perform." The dream and its narration set in motion a chain of events that were not disasters but the work of grace. All events that

touch us are aids to God's purpose of conforming us to the image of his Son.[9]

In The Pit

Due to their envy and hatred for Joseph, while they were out tending the flock at Shechem, his brothers said, "let us now kill him." It was Rueben that talked them out of such a horrible deed. He convinced them to throw Joseph in a pit and then ultimately sell him to some Midianite traders for twenty pieces of silver. They took the coat of his father's favor and dipped it in goat blood and carried it to Israel and told them that a wild beast had killed his favored son.

Joseph has a choice to make at that very moment. Does he become angry, bitter, and resentful toward his brothers? Does he doubt the dream God had given him? Or does he maintain faith in God and believe that if he holds a heavenly protocol keeping all things in perspective, God's dream and destiny will come to pass.

The pit experience of Joseph is a reminder of how much it may cost to follow your dream. He shared his dream at the wrong time with the wrong crowd, and it cost him his freedom. It's essential to be mindful of the time and place to share your dreams. Not everyone will be happy to hear your dreams, and that may include your own family, (see Genesis 37:18-20).

What can we learn from the pit? In a split second, Joseph's life was changed from being the beloved son to being tossed into a pit to die. One minute he's wearing the coat of favor, and the next, he's not sure he will see another sunrise. The enemy wants to trap us in a pit of hopelessness and despair, thinking that God has forsaken us. We know that God is for us in our hearts, but it's difficult to latch on to God's

---

[9] Donald Grey Barnhouse, *Genesis, Two Volumes in One,* (Grand Rapids, MI: Zondervan Publishing House, 1970). p. 158.

promises when we are surrounded by betrayal from our very own family.

It's one thing to be in the pit with all of its difficulties, but we must be watchful of certain pitfalls while in the struggle.

Five Pitfalls That Joseph Might Have Faced.

1. Thinking the pit was punishment for something he did wrong—he wasn't being punished.
2. Thinking the pit was permanent—it was only a temporary holding place on his way to the fulfillment of his dreams.
3. Festering bitterness toward his brothers.
4. Falling into despair with no end in sight—except death.
5. Resentment toward God for allowing such madness to happen.

The dreams were meant to be his anchor when times became difficult. They would not take away the pain, but they would keep his hope alive. In the same way, God gives us promises through his Word or by speaking to us directly. His words will anchor us because there will be times when we need to revisit them to sustain our hope. When we know deep inside that God gave us a promise, it will carry us through the challenges.[10]

Potiphar's House

The favor on Joseph's life was a blessing and a curse all at the same time. He was purchased as a slave by Potiphar, a captain of the

---

[10] *The Purpose in Your Pain: Lessons From Joseph,* http://someinspiredthoughts.com; accessed July 1, 2021.

guard of Pharaoh. There was such favor upon Joseph that Potiphar made him ruler of his house.

> *The Lord was with Joseph, and he was a successful man; and he was in the house of his master the Egyptian. And his master saw that the Lord was with him and that the Lord made all he did to prosper in his hand. ⁴ So Joseph found favor in his sight, and served him. Then he made him overseer of his house, and all that he had he put under his authority. So it was, from the time that he had made him overseer of his house and all that he had, that the Lord blessed the Egyptian's house for Joseph's sake; and the blessing of the Lord was on all that he had in the house and in the field.*
>
> Genesis 39:2-5 (NKJV)

But the same favor caused Potiphar's wife to be attracted to Joseph, and she wanted him to sleep with her. He ran for his life, leaving his coat in her hand. She then lies about Joseph and claims he tried to rape her.

Well, that little ordeal lands him in prison.

> *But it happened about this time, when Joseph went into the house to do his work, and none of the men of the house was inside, that she caught him by his garment, saying, "Lie with me." But he left his garment in her hand, and fled and ran outside. And so it was, when she saw that he had left his garment in her hand and fled outside, that she called to the men of her house and spoke to them, saying, "See, he has brought in to us a Hebrew to mock us. He came in to me to lie with me, and I cried out with a loud voice. And it happened, when he heard that I lifted my voice and cried out, that*

> *he left his garment with me, and fled and went outside."*
>
> *So she kept his garment with her until his master came home. Then she spoke to him with words like these, saying, "The Hebrew servant whom you brought to us came in to me to mock me; so it happened, as I lifted my voice and cried out, that he left his garment with me and fled outside."*

Genesis 39:11-18 (NKJV)

Bible Teacher Andrew Wommack observed, "Joseph was able to maintain his integrity because he was not concerned with what man thought. He did not consider the benefits or consequences of his actions based on what Potiphar, his master, might do. Notice his reasoning in Genesis 39:9, it says, 'How then can I do this great wickedness, and sin against God?'"[11]

Prison

It seems to this preacher that if Potiphar believed what his wife had told him, he would have had Joseph tortured and killed. But he put Joseph in prison instead. I don't think for a minute that his first days in prison were like summer camp. Psalm 105:17-22 explains the full impact of how much Joseph's integrity meant to him. He was willing to suffer for his convictions.

> *He sent a man before them—*
> *Joseph—who was sold as a slave.*
> *They hurt his feet with fetters,*
> *He was laid in irons.*
> *Until the time that his word came to pass,*
> *The word of the Lord tested him.*

---

[11] Andrew Wommack Ministries, *Lessons from Joseph,* https://www.awmi.net/reading/teaching-articles/lessons_joseph/ accessed July 1, 2021.

> *The king sent and released him,*
> *The ruler of the people let him go free.*
> *He made him lord of his house,*
> *And ruler of all his possessions,*
> *To bind his princes at his pleasure,*
> *And teach his elders wisdom.*
>
> Psalm 105:17-22 (NKJV)

Despite the false charges leveled against him, God's favor followed Joseph into the prison.

> *So it was, when his master heard the words which his wife spoke to him, saying, "Your servant did to me after this manner," that his anger was aroused. Then Joseph's master took him and put him into the prison, a place where the king's prisoners were confined. And he was there in the prison.* **But the Lord was with Joseph and showed him mercy, and He gave him favor in the sight of the keeper of the prison** *[emphasis mine].* *And the keeper of the prison committed to Joseph's hand all the prisoners who were in the prison; whatever they did there, it was his doing. The keeper of the prison did not look into anything that was under Joseph's authority,* **because the Lord was with him; and whatever he did, the Lord made it prosper.** *[emphasis mine]*
>
> Genesis 39:19-23 (NKJV)

But that's not the end of the story.

The butler and baker of the king of Egypt ended up being thrown into the same prison as Joseph. One night each of them had a dream. Joseph interpreted their dreams, telling them accurately that the chief butler would be set free within three days, but the chief baker would be hanged. Joseph had a simple request of the butler— "please remember me and mention me to Pharaoh."

How Did I End Up Here?

The turning point came when Joseph was summoned to go before Pharaoh and interpret a dream that his servants could not interpret. The butler remembered Joseph and recommended to Pharaoh that he give Joseph a try. Joseph rightly interpreted Pharaoh's dream. He said that seven years of plenty would be followed by seven years of famine. Joseph interpreted this dream to save the entire world that day and make Pharaoh the wealthiest and most powerful man in the world. That's why Pharaoh said what he did about Joseph when he said, "Inasmuch as God has shown you all this, there is no one as discerning and wise as you."

An important point that we must make is before Joseph went in to see the Pharaoh, he shaved and changed clothes. Why did he do that? It was totally against his culture and religion. He knew to be taken seriously and to have an opportunity to be promoted by Pharaoh; Joseph had to show that even though he was a Hebrew, he was willing to adapt to the Pharaoh's culture because he would be representing him.

At The Palace

Interestingly, Joseph's journey followed a seven-step protocol. I have discovered that these seven steps run concurrently throughout scripture in the life of every person God used, including Jesus. Let's Look at Joseph's protocol.

1. ALIGNMENT

Joseph looked at each stop in his life along the way as a promotion. Even when it didn't look like it on the surface. He would have died if he'd stayed in Canaan. He always aligned with whoever his leader was.

2. AUTHORITY

Joseph submitted to every authority God put over him because he knew that alignment establishes the parameters of one's authority. He learned to have authority he would have to be under authority. Why? Because authority receives its power to operate in its assignment through submission.

3. DOMINION

Authority is given to the one properly aligned to establish dominion in the realm of their assignment. Joseph was aligned with Pharaoh, who happened to be the wealthiest, most powerful man in the world. Because he submitted to his authority, he was given dominion over the entire kingdom.

4. VISION

Vision is receiving Holy Spirit revelation and releasing it into your assignment. Joseph knew that he had been sent to Egypt to save Israel during a seven-year famine. That's why he told his brothers when they came to see him.

> *But now, do not therefore be grieved or angry with yourselves because you sold me here; for God sent me before you to preserve life. For these two years the famine has been in the land, and there are still five years in which there will be neither plowing nor harvesting. And God sent me before you to preserve a posterity for you in the earth, and to save your lives by a great deliverance. So now it was not you who sent me here, but God; and He has made me a father to Pharaoh, and lord of all his house, and a ruler throughout all the land of Egypt.*
>
> Genesis 45:5-8 (NKJV)

5. CREATIVITY

Joseph is now in his element, aligned under Pharaoh, submitted to his authority. Joseph has taken dominion over the known world and uses God's vision for his life and the world to be creative in saving Israel. He didn't just save Israel and his entire family, either. He put them in the land of Goshen. The most fertile land in all the regions where they wouldn't just get by but prosper greatly.

6. PURPOSE

Now you have arrived at your destiny. Your purpose is what you have been put on earth to fulfill. Joseph made it to the very reason he was put on this earth. Now you are ready for step seven.

7. PROMOTION

You'll never move on to your next level of assignment until you fulfill the purpose of your last assignment; in Joseph's case, that was to tell his children to take his bones back to the land of Promise. And they did.

> *And Joseph said to his brethren, "I am dying; but God will surely visit you, and bring you out of this land to the land of which He swore to Abraham, to Isaac, and to Jacob." Then Joseph took an oath from the children of Israel, saying, "God will surely visit you, and you shall carry up my bones from here." So Joseph died, being one hundred and ten years old; and they embalmed him, and he was put in a coffin in Egypt.*
>
> Genesis 50:24-26 (NKJV)

A Final Thought

Obeying God where you are rather than living a life resenting those who betrayed you is what allows God to use you in the supernatural. Joseph was used to prophesy into the life and ministry of Jesus. At the time of Jacob's death, he laid hands on all of his sons. He said to them, "Gather together, that I may tell you what shall befall you in the last days" Genesis 49:1 (NKJV).

Jacob continued in verses 22-25 as he prophesied a future event connected to the life of Joseph.

> *Joseph is a fruitful bough,*
> *A fruitful bough by a well;*
> *His branches run over the wall.*

Betrayal

> *The archers have bitterly grieved him,*
> *Shot at him and hated him.*
> *But his bow remained in strength,*
> *And the arms of his hands were made strong*
> *By the hands of the Mighty God of Jacob*
> *(From there is the Shepherd, the Stone of Israel),*
> *By the God of your father who will help you,*
> *And by the Almighty who will bless you*
> *With blessings of heaven above,*
> *Blessings of the deep that lies beneath,*
> *Blessings of the breasts and of the womb.*
>
> Genesis 49:22-25 (NKJV)

Many Bible teachers, myself included, believe what Jacob said in Joseph's blessing is also a Messianic prophecy fulfilled in the life of Jesus in John 4. Notice John 4:5 does not say Jesus met a woman at Jacob's well, but rather at "the well Jacob gave his son Joseph." And he did so at Sychar, which is in ancient Shechem, the very place where Joseph was sold into slavery.

I want to render for you a partial interpretation and paraphrase of Genesis 49:22-24.

> *Joseph My favored Son whom I am constantly adding to his life, is a fruitful Son (bough) even a fruitful Son by the eye or head of the fountain of waters (well) whose daughter (branches) runs over tearing down a wall!*
>
> *Baal (archers) shot arrows of bitterness trickling in and married those who lay in wait to destroy Him.*
>
> *But his weapon (bow) sat down (remained) in permanence (strength), and He became the (zeroar) arm of the Lord God Himself from His closed hand came the Shepherd, the Cornerstone of Israel!*

> *The God of Israel will surround you, and El Shaddai will kneel before you and bless (Benediction) call finished over your life what El Shaddai has promised. He has promised a fountain of waters that comes from the overflowing compassion of a woman's womb and her child.*
>
> *The blessings of Israel have exceeded the blessings of Abraham and Isaac and will deliver the fulfillment of one who is the Ancient of Days coming from the hills, and He shall become the High Priest of Israel, and the King separated or set apart from his brethren.*

Now watch.

This scripture was fulfilled in John 4 (not at Jacob's well), but John 4:5 called it Joseph's well. And, He through a fountain of water used a daughter, a woman, a gentile to tear down a wall creating One New Man delivering peace.

Notice Joseph is a fruitful son by a well whose daughter runs over a wall tearing it down. God used a Gentile woman to tear down a wall of religion by a well that not only saved her but opened the Gospel up to all Gentiles.

It's the message of the One New Man spoken of in Ephesians 2.

> *Therefore remember that you, once Gentiles in the flesh—who are called Uncircumcision by what is called the Circumcision made in the flesh by hands—that at that time you were without Christ, being aliens from the commonwealth of Israel and strangers from the covenants of promise, having no hope and without God in the world. But now in Christ Jesus you who once were far off have been brought near by the blood of Christ.*

> *For He Himself is our peace, who has made both one, and has broken down the middle wall of separation, having abolished in His flesh the enmity, that is, the law of commandments contained in ordinances, so as to create in Himself one new man from the two, thus making peace, and that He might reconcile them both to God in one body through the cross, thereby putting to death the enmity. And He came and preached peace to you who were afar off and to those who were near. For through Him we both have access by one Spirit to the Father.*
>
> Ephesians 2:11-18 (NKJV)

This is why Jesus said to the woman at the well in John 4:10 (NKJV), "If you knew the gift of God, and who it is who says to you, 'Give Me a drink,' you would have asked Him, and He would have given you living water."

This also prophetically demonstrates that the Gospel is with the Gentiles for two days or two thousand years. Then on the third day, or in the third millennium, after Jesus' death, the Gospel would return to the Jews; because Jesus stayed with the Samaritans for two days but then returned to the Jews on the third day.

As I stated at the beginning of this chapter, Joseph is the Old Testament type of Christ. The comparisons are hard to miss. For instance…

- Both were the object of their father's love. (Genesis 37:3; Matthew 3:17).

- Both were betrayed for silver. (Genesis 37:28; Matthew 26:15).

- Both embraced pain to walk in their destiny. (Genesis 45:5-8; Matthew 26:39).

- Both were entrusted with ALL things. (Genesis 39:4-8; John 3:35).
- Both suffered to save many. (Genesis 50:21; John 3:16).
- Both were made rulers. (Genesis 41:42-44; Matthew 28:18).
- Both were falsely accused. (Genesis 39:19-20; Mark 14:56).
- Both set the example of how to handle betrayal. (Genesis 45:5-8; Luke 23:34).

5

Guard Your Heart and Your Secrets

Samson Betrayed by Delilah

An affection which is not inspired by the Lord will soon be transformed into lust. Samson is not alone in the history of man in failing in this regard. Delilah is still cutting the hair of man today!

Watchman Nee

> *Keep your heart with all diligence, For out of it spring the issues of life.*
>
> Proverbs 4:23

Several years ago, my wife, Amy, and a few other members of my family visited the Sight & Sound Theatre in Branson, Missouri. We were there to view the theatrical production of Samson. It proved to be by far one of the best live performances we've ever seen. At the same time, I was reintroduced to the life of a Bible character named Samson. He was so powerful that God listed him in his Hall of Fame of Faith.

> *And what more shall I say? For the time would fail me to tell of Gideon and Barak and Samson and Jephthah, also of David and Samuel and the prophets: who through*

> *faith subdued kingdoms, worked righteousness, obtained promises, stopped the mouths of lions, quenched the violence of fire, escaped the edge of the sword, out of weakness were made strong, became valiant in battle, turned to flight the armies of the aliens.*
>
> Hebrews 11:32-34 (NKJV)

You might be thinking, "But didn't Samson die in shame?" No, technically, he died in faith. The unfortunate truth of Samson's life is that his anointing—his strength—was ultimately his downfall. The power God gave him caused him to believe he was invincible. Over time he learned that only God is invincible, and everyone is replaceable, including the strongest man on the planet.

Consider Samson's Past

An angel of the Lord appeared to Samson's mother—we aren't given her name—just that she was Manoah's wife and that she was barren. The angel promised her a son.

> *Behold you shall conceive and bear a son. Now drink no wine or similar drink, nor eat anything unclean, for the child shall be a Nazarite to God from the womb to the day of his death.*
>
> Judges 13:7 (NKJV)

Since Manoah didn't hear the original message, he prayed and asked God to resend the angel; and the Lord answered his prayer. Manoah receives the word and instruction firsthand from the angel. He proceeds to offer a sacrifice on a rock altar, and God consumed it with a flame of fire, and the angel went up to heaven in the flame.

Notice that the angel was very precise about Samson's future— "for the child shall be a Nazarite to God from the womb to the day of his death." The Nazirite vow was a serious matter. Numbers chapter six describes three commitments a Nazirite must keep.

> *Then the Lord spoke to Moses, saying, "Speak to the children of Israel, and say to them: 'When either a man or woman consecrates an offering to take the vow of a Nazirite, to separate himself to the Lord, **he shall separate himself from wine and similar drink;** he shall drink neither vinegar made from wine nor vinegar made from similar drink; neither shall he drink any grape juice, nor eat fresh grapes or raisins. All the days of his separation he shall eat nothing that is produced by the grapevine, from seed to skin.*
>
> ***All the days of the vow of his separation no razor shall come upon his head;*** *until the days are fulfilled for which he separated himself to the Lord, he shall be holy. Then he shall let the locks of the hair of his head grow.* ***All the days that he separates himself to the Lord he shall not go near a dead body.*** *He shall not make himself unclean even for his father or his mother, for his brother or his sister, when they die, because his separation to God is on his head. All the days of his separation he shall be holy to the Lord. [emphasis mine].*
>
> Numbers 6:1-8 (NKJV)

The three commitments a Nazirite must keep during their vow are very specific and must be followed, with no exceptions.

1. Avoid any contact with grapes or the consumption of wine.
2. Let your hair grow, and never allow it to be cut.
3. Never touch a dead body of any kind.

Manoah's wife bore a son, just as the angel had said, and she named him Samson. His name means, "sunshine." Keep in mind at the time of Samson's birth, the children of Israel were in captivity by the Philistines because of their disobedience. They needed some sunshine or a ray of hope to bring liberty out of their bondage; and, from all appearances, Samson was their guy. But notice a very telling statement in Judges 13:5 (NKJV), "and he shall begin to deliver Israel out of the hand of the Philistines." [emphasis mine].

Samson was no doubt the strongest man in the world at the time and maybe of all time. But with the increase in his strength, there was also an increase in his arrogance and carelessness. As we see the story of Samson unfold, it will become evident, even to the casual observer, that Samson never actually delivered Israel from bondage to the Philistines. Why? Because he was never delivered himself.

As Samson grew older, his eye for the ladies became apparent. He asked his parents to arrange for him to marry a certain woman from Timnah, a Philistine. His parents didn't realize that it was a God-given plan to get Samson closer to the enemy of Israel, the hated Philistines. The Bible tells us that while Samson waited on his parents in a vineyard, a young lion attacked him.

> *And the Spirit of the Lord came mightily upon him, and he tore the lion apart as one would have torn apart a young goat, though he had nothing in his hand. But he did not tell his father or his mother what he had done.*
>
> Judges 14:6 (NKJV)

One day on his way to visit the Philistine in Timnah, he passed by the carcass of the lion he had killed, and some bees had built a hive inside. Samson reached in and took some honeycomb and ate it. He carried some to his parents, and they ate it, but Samson did not tell his parents where he got the honey. Do you notice a pattern here? Samson is not transparent with the people who love him the most. The most dangerous thing in a man's life is to gain strength and success with no accountability. Everyone must be accountable to someone. I was told by a minister one time that no one was qualified to be over him or correct him. If anyone in leadership ever tells you that is their philosophy—don't just leave; run as fast as you can.

Did you also notice that Samson broke the three commitments of the Nazarite vow in a short period?

1. He goes into a vineyard (Judges 14:5; Numbers 6:3).
2. He touched a dead carcass (Judges 14:8-9; Numbers 6:6).
3. He made a feast "as was customary for bridegrooms." The word for *feast* means, "a drinking party." (Judges 14:10; Numbers 6:2).

Samson seems to be more concerned about the ladies than he is about his commitment to God. As one pastor commented, "Samson was hormone-driven, not Holy Spirit driven!"

Samson Takes Revenge

The Spirit of the Lord began to move on Samson. He had become a judge over Israel. Samson was a brilliant and wise man over many things. His feats are legendary, but it's his flaws that will overwhelm him and bring him down.

The cracks in his character begin to show.

One day at what was likely his wedding feast in Timnah, he made up a riddle for 30 of the young Philistine men that were there at the celebration. These were hired partiers, not friends but professional celebrators. Feeling invincible and overconfident, he posed a bet. If they could answer his riddle, he would give all 30 of the men a new suit of clothes. If they could not solve the riddle, they would have to provide him with 30 new suits of clothes. Here is the riddle; "Out of the eater came something to eat, and out of the strong came something sweet." Samson gave them seven days to answer. After three days of not figuring out the answer, they approached his wife and gave her an ultimatum. She could get the answer from Samson and tell them, or they would burn her and her father's house down. Samson's wife did what a lot of ladies do in this situation. She turned on the waterworks. She went to Samson and exclaimed, "You hate me! You don't love me!

If you loved me you would tell me the answer to the riddle!" (See Judges 14:15-18).

And as it usually does, it worked. She wore Samson down, and on day seven; he told her the answer. When Samson came to collect his winnings, he was shocked to hear the answer to his riddle. The men proclaimed, "What is sweeter than honey, and what is stronger than a lion?" Samson's response is priceless; he said, "If you had not plowed with my heifer you would not have solved my riddle." He was not a wise man to call his wife a heifer.

What was Samson's reaction?

Then the Spirit of the Lord came upon him mightily, and he went down to Ashkelon and killed thirty of their men, took their apparel, and gave the changes of clothing to those who had explained the riddle. So his anger was aroused, and he went back up to his father's house. ***And Samson's wife was given to his companion, who had been his best man.*** *[emphasis mine].*

Judges 14:19-20 (NKJV)

Samson showed up at his father-in-law's and is told that his wife was given to his best man. (See Judges 15). If your new bride is given away to your best man, you have a solid case to develop a bad attitude. And that is exactly what happened to Samson. Samson is informed that he could have her younger sister instead, and it becomes painfully evident that Samson did not take the news well.

Samson's attitude goes from bad to worse. "This time I shall be blameless regarding the Philistines if I harm them." Judges 15:3 (NKJV). In other words, do not blame me for what I am about to do! Samson never got over what happened with his first wife. So, what did he do? He made a terrible decision based on his pain, and that never works out well.

Samson is not the first—think of Eve who blamed the snake—and he won't be the last to blame someone or some unforeseen circumstance for their ungodly behavior. Shifting blame has become a national pastime with many people. Why is that? It's just so much easier to find someone to blame than to take personal responsibility for your actions.

He caught 300 foxes in his anger, and he tied their tails together with a torch in between them. He then turned them loose in the wheat fields that were ready to harvest. He burned up all the grain fields, the vineyards, and olive groves. In retaliation, the Philistines burned Samson's wife and father-in-law to death.

Next, Samson attacked the Philistines who did this and slaughtered them all. The Bible uses the expression that Samson "attacked them hip and thigh," Judges 15:8 (NKJV), an old proverbial saying that means, "great and mighty." It's safe to say that when you ticked, "ol' sunshine off," he would rain on your parade.

Samson now finds himself hiding in the cleft of the rock of Etam about 15 to 20 feet below the surface (according to Barnes Notes) in Judah or Southern Israel. It took 3000 men of Judah to arrest Samson and then turn him over to the Philistines.

What happens next is a story of all stories.

> *When he came to Lehi, the Philistines came shouting against him. Then the Spirit of the Lord came mightily upon him; and the ropes that were on his arms became like flax that is burned with fire, and his bonds broke loose from his hands. He found a fresh jawbone of a donkey, reached out his hand and took it, and killed a thousand men with it. Then Samson said:*
>
> *"With the jawbone of a donkey,*
> *Heaps upon heaps,*
> *With the jawbone of a donkey*
> *I have slain a thousand men!"*

And so it was, when he had finished speaking, that he threw the jawbone from his hand, and called that place Ramath Lehi.

Then he became very thirsty; so he cried out to the Lord and said, "You have given this great deliverance by the hand of Your servant; and now shall I die of thirst and fall into the hand of the uncircumcised?" So God split the hollow place that is in Lehi, and water came out, and he drank; and his spirit returned, and he revived. Therefore he called its name En Hakkore, which is in Lehi to this day. And he judged Israel twenty years in the days of the Philistines.

Judges 15:14-20 (NKJV)

Betrayal

Sadly, this man who was so powerfully anointed and had so much going for him is only known for his relationship with a woman named Delilah. I doubt that Samson would have believed that his life and his betrayal by Delilah would be plastered on the big screen or made into a play that my wife and I would watch thousands of years after the event took place.

Samson's lifestyle, cockiness, and arrogance are getting worse. He goes to meet a harlot in Gaza. The men of the city lay in wait for him to come out the following morning. But Samson fools them and comes out at midnight instead, and he rips the doors of the city gate, the fence posts, and bars right off the city wall and carries them to the top of a hill.

Now Samson went to Gaza and saw a harlot there, and went in to her. When the Gazites were told, "Samson has come here!" they surrounded the place and lay in wait for him all night at the gate of the city. They were quiet all night, saying, "In the morning, when it is daylight, we will kill him." And Samson lay low till

> *midnight; then he arose at midnight, took hold of the doors of the gate of the city and the two gateposts, pulled them up, bar and all, put them on his shoulders, and carried them to the top of the hill that faces Hebron.*
>
> Judges 16:1-3 (NKJV)

Now, the Philistines are so desperate to kill him that they enlist a harlot named Delilah. They demand that she find out the source of Samson's strength, and if successful, they will pay her 1100 pieces of silver.

If I had to pinpoint where Samson's arrogance was going to finally catch up with him, it would be his disastrous relationship with Delilah. Why? He is about to open his heart to the one person he needed to run from; but, instead of running away—remember Joseph—he chose to share his innermost secrets. He is about to experience the highest form of betrayal, and it comes from the woman he loves.

The name Delilah means, "weakness or brought low." Samson was no stranger to the "ladies of the night," but Delilah was the first woman that made him pliable like warm moldable clay in her hands.

Delilah pleads with him to tell her his secret.

He plays with her emotions.

But he will give in…

The three moving parts in this story each had their motivation as follows: Firstly, Samson was in it for love—maybe for the first time in his life. Secondly, Delilah's head was turned, not by Samson, but by the offer of money to betray him. And thirdly, the Philistines were motivated by power and control. This trifecta of girls, gold, and glory has been the downfall of many men—especially those in ministry.

> *And Samson said to her, "If they bind me with seven fresh bowstrings, not yet dried, then I shall become*

weak, and be like any other man." So the lords of the Philistines brought up to her seven fresh bowstrings, not yet dried, and she bound him with them. Now men were lying in wait, staying with her in the room. And she said to him, "The Philistines are upon you, Samson!" But he broke the bowstrings as a strand of yarn breaks when it touches fire. So the secret of his strength was not known.

Then Delilah said to Samson, "Look, you have mocked me and told me lies. Now, please tell me what you may be bound with." So he said to her, "If they bind me securely with new ropes that have never been used, then I shall become weak, and be like any other man."

Therefore Delilah took new ropes and bound him with them, and said to him, "The Philistines are upon you, Samson!" And men were lying in wait, staying in the room. But he broke them off his arms like a thread. Delilah said to Samson, "Until now you have mocked me and told me lies. Tell me what you may be bound with."

And he said to her, "If you weave the seven locks of my head into the web of the loom"—So she wove it tightly with the batten of the loom, and said to him, "The Philistines are upon you, Samson!" But he awoke from his sleep, and pulled out the batten and the web from the loom. Then she said to him, "How can you say, 'I love you,' when your heart is not with me?

*You have mocked me these three times, and have not told me where your great strength lies." And it came to pass, when she pestered him daily with her words and pressed him**, so that his soul was vexed to death,***

> *that he told her all his heart, and said to her, "No razor has ever come upon my head, for I have been a Nazirite to God from my mother's womb. If I am shaven, then my strength will leave me, and I shall become weak, and be like any other man."*
>
> *When Delilah saw that he had told her all his heart, she sent and called for the lords of the Philistines, saying, "Come up once more, for he has told me all his heart." [emphasis mine]. So the lords of the Philistines came up to her and brought the money in their hand. Then she lulled him to sleep on her knees, and called for a man and had him shave off the seven locks of his head. Then she began to torment him, and his strength left him. And she said, "The Philistines are upon you, Samson!" So he awoke from his sleep, and said, "I will go out as before, at other times, and shake myself free!" But he did not know that the Lord had departed from him.*
>
> *Then the Philistines took him and put out his eyes, and brought him down to Gaza. They bound him with bronze fetters, and he became a grinder in the prison.*
>
> Judges 16:7-21 (NKJV)

I find a touch of humor in the statement that Delilah pestered and pressed him until his soul became vexed to death. The word vexed means irritated, distressed, or annoyed. Samson learned a hard lesson that all of us need to know; the enemy will make sure to send certain people in our life to vex us. Even Samson's strength could not insulate him from becoming so irritated with her that he gave in to her demand.

The Bible teaches to "Keep [guard] your heart with all diligence, for out of it spring the issues of life" (Proverbs 4:23 NKJV). It makes sense to believe that when Samson gave away his secrets to Delilah, he

Betrayal

also gave her his heart. Be very careful, my friend with whom you share your secrets—it could cost you everything.

This story of Samson brings back a memory of an anecdote that the late Dr. Adrian Rogers said about the story of Samson: He said, "Sin will take you farther than you want to go. Sin will keep you longer than you want to stay. And sin will cost you more than you will want to pay." I say AMEN to that!

If this is the story of Samson and his betrayal by Delilah, how did he end up in God's Hall of Fame of Faith? From all indications, he looked like a loser to me.

- Samson had experienced the blinding power of sin.
- Samson had experienced the binding power of sin.
- And, he had experienced the grinding power of sin.

His days of judging Israel and defeating her enemies were over. He had been reduced to nothing more than an animal. Judges 16:21 (NKJV) says, "Then the Philistines took him and put out his eyes, and brought him down to Gaza. They bound him with bronze fetters, and he became a grinder in the prison."

But that's not the end of the story!

The beginning of the end is laid out for us in Judges 16:22 (NKJV). "However the hair of his head began to grow again after it had been shaven."

Was his hair the source of his strength? No, absolutely not! The Bible says repeatedly, "The Spirit of the Lord came mightily upon him." That was the source of his strength. But Samson had been told by his mother that his hair was his strength. Now his hair is growing back, and so is his belief.

> *Now the lords of the Philistines gathered together to offer a great sacrifice to Dagon their god, and to rejoice. And they said:*

"Our god has delivered into our hands Samson our enemy!"

When the people saw him, they praised their god; for they said:

"Our god has delivered into our hands our enemy, The destroyer of our land, And the one who multiplied our dead."

So it happened, when their hearts were merry, that they said, "Call for Samson, that he may perform for us." So they called for Samson from the prison, and he performed for them. And they stationed him between the pillars. Then Samson said to the lad who held him by the hand, "Let me feel the pillars which support the temple, so that I can lean on them." Now the temple was full of men and women. All the lords of the Philistines were there—about three thousand men and women on the roof watching while Samson performed.

Then Samson called to the Lord, saying, "O Lord God, remember me, I pray! Strengthen me, I pray, just this once, O God, that I may with one blow take vengeance on the Philistines for my two eyes!" And Samson took hold of the two middle pillars which supported the temple, and he braced himself against them, one on his right and the other on his left. Then Samson said, "Let me die with the Philistines!" And he pushed with all his might, and the temple fell on the lords and all the people who were in it. So the dead that he killed at his death were more than he had killed in his life.

And his brothers and all his father's household came down and took him, and brought him up and buried him between Zorah and Eshtaol in the tomb of his father Manoah. He had judged Israel twenty years.

Judges 16:23-31 (NKJV)

A Final Thought

In the end, Samson's faith in the face of his failure proved to be the source of his strength. He learned something that we all must learn; when we are faced with failure; "Faith is our acceptance of God's acceptance of us despite everything."

One of my favorite authors, Dr. Brene Brown, says, "Shame is the swampland of the soul." She also says that "Vulnerability is the most accurate measurement of courage."[12] Samson may have ended up living in the "swampland of the soul," but he died in courage, and God put him in His Hall of Fame of Faith.

I like to say, "If shame is the swampland of the soul, then regret is the quicksand." Either way, you have to get out of shame and regret to do anything great for God.

Pastor John Lowe observed:

Notice how the story ends in verse 30: "Then he pushed with all his might, and down came the temple on the rulers and all the people in it. Thus he killed many more when he died than while he lived." You will find that to be true in your life, if you are willing to go back to the place of disobedience and face it. Reckon yourself to be dead to sin and alive to God. God will then crush the Philistines in your life.

Do you want to know the moral to this story? It really has nothing to do with Samson and everything to do with God. This passage is a living lesson in the grace of God. How a man who was beaten and blinded, humiliated by his own

---

[12] Dr. Brene Brown quotes, accessed on July 25, 2021, https://julietvanheerden.com/2014/04/04/shame-and-vulnerability-unmasked/

repeated stupidity, reached the bottom, turned around, and discovered that God was waiting for him all the time.

There's nothing heroic about Samson. All he did was turn around and find God. God is the hero. Some of us need to hear this. Maybe you've gone pretty far down the road of romance or revenge and you're grinding under a load of guilt.

Listen carefully. Restoration of a relationship with God does not depend upon your performance. How can I say that? Because Samson didn't perform. He came back to God before he pushed those pillars down. He came back to God while he was still shackled. He came back to God while he was still blind. He turned back to God and God took him.[13]

> *Looking unto Jesus the author and finisher of our faith, who for the joy that was set before Him endured the cross, despising the shame, and has sat down at the right hand of the throne of God.*
>
> Hebrews 12:2 (NKJV)

The phrase despising the shame means HE SHAMED SHAME!

Samson discovered a valuable lesson through all of the victories, defeats, and betrayals: have faith, not in yourself, and not in the length of your hair.

Like Samson, we too can have confidence in the one who paid for all our shame and regret and can still use us to defeat His and our enemies.

---

[13] Pastor John Lowe, *Dealing with Fatal Flaws,* accessed on July 25, 2021, https://www.sermoncentral.com/sermons/samson-dealing-with-fatal-flaws-john-lowe-sermon-on-samson-233005?page=1&wc=800

6

All Alone in a Dark Place

John the Baptist felt betrayed by Jesus

John the Baptist never performed any miracles. Yet, he was greater than any of the Old Testament prophets.

Leonard Ravenhill

After Jesus had finished instructing his twelve disciples, he went on from there to teach and preach in the towns of Galilee. When John, who was in prison, heard about the deeds of the Messiah, he sent his disciples to ask him, "Are you the one who is to come, or should we expect someone else?"

Jesus replied, "Go back and report to John what you hear and see: The blind receive sight, the lame walk, those who have leprosy are cleansed, the deaf hear, the dead are raised, and the good news is proclaimed to the poor. Blessed is anyone who does not stumble on account of me."

Matthew 11:1-6

John the Baptist was one of the most influential men who ever walked the earth. Jesus said this about him.

Truly I tell you, among those born of women there has not risen anyone greater than John the Baptist; yet whoever is least in the kingdom of heaven is greater than he.

Matthew 11:11

I would say that Jesus gave John a strong endorsement, wouldn't you? John is about to learn a crucial lesson…life is not fair. And circumstances don't always turn out the way you think they should.

In the life of a believer, you will find all kinds of tension.

- The way up is down.
- If you want to be first, be last.
- If you want to lead, learn to serve.
- In order to live, you must die.
- In order to get, you must give.
- If you want to rise to the top, start at the bottom.
- You're in the world, not of it.
- The gap between what we see around us and what we know inside of us.
- And so much more!

And that brings us to John the baptizer.

As we read the account in Matthew 11, we discover that John has a problem. His circumstances are at war with his calling, and he does the only thing he knows to do—he reaches out to Jesus.

When John sent his disciples to question Jesus, he knew that death was imminent. His head is about to be cut off, and he wanted reassurance from Jesus that a rescue was imminent. I don't blame him. John was saying, are you worth dying for? I can hear him praying,

Father, is this happening? Are you going to let me die alone in a dark place?

I believe John knew in his heart that there would come a time when he would have to die for his calling. But, when you are all alone in a dark place, a dungeon, staring at a sword that's about to cut your head off, it's easy to see why John senses that maybe he has been betrayed. And his betrayal was not by some disciple who tagged along but by the Lamb of God himself.

Have you ever felt betrayed by the Father for doing what He's called you to do?

You are not alone.

Consider the story of a Swedish couple, David and Svea Flood.

In 1921, a Swedish couple, David and Svea Flood, felt called by God to go as missionaries to the Belgian Congo. They took with them their two-year-old son. At a mission station, they met another couple, the Ericksons, and targeted a remote village where the Gospel of Christ had never been preached. Things started to get tough when the chief of that village refused to grant them permission to live with them and to talk about Jesus. At first, the missionaries remained undeterred. They built mud huts about a half-mile away and prayed for an open door. The only person from the village they had contact with was a young boy who sold them chickens and eggs. David and Svea prayed that if God would not allow them to convert the village, he would at least allow them to lead this one boy to Christ. God honored that prayer, and the young boy became a Christian. The Erickson's left and went back to the mission station. The Floods, however, remained in their hut waiting for the village to open up to them. It never did. Svea Flood was pregnant and gave birth to a little girl, whom they named Anna. Svea had been sick with malaria and other tropical diseases and, 17 days after the birth of her daughter, she died. At that point, something snapped in her husband David. He turned his back on his calling and God. He went to the mission station, gave his daughter to the Erickson's, and returned to Sweden with his son. Little Anna wound up with American missionaries who brought her back to the United States and raised her in South Dakota. She became a Christian and, years later, came across a photograph of her birth mother's crude grave in the Belgian Congo. Anna knew the story of her birth and learned more about the rest of the story. The little boy whom the Floods converted to Christ went away to school and returned as an educator to his village. He started a school there and won every student to Christ. The students took the Gospel home to their parents and eventually there were six hundred converts to Christ in that single village. Even the old chief himself became a Christian. Anna and her husband went to Sweden in search of her birth father. He had remarried and had four other children but had become an alcoholic and was separated from his second family by the time she met him. Her father was old and near death when Anna came into his room. She had been warned not to talk about God. Her father was so embittered that he would not allow the name of God to be mentioned in his house. Anna stepped into the room and said "Papa." He turned on his bed and said, "Anna, my Anna, I never meant to give you away." She replied, "It's all right, Papa. God worked it for good." He stiffened and said, "Don't say that name, He took everything from me." She said, "No, Papa, God did not take everything from you. Your work was not in vain; Mama's work was not in vain." Then she told of the little boy who led six hundred people to Christ in the village. Her embittered father's heart melted and he began to sob. Eventually, Anna's father came back to Christ in the weeks before he died. Anna felt great joy that she could be used by God in this way. A couple of years later, Anna and her husband attended an international conference in England. Representatives were there from all over the world. A young man was there from the Belgian Congo (which, as you know, was later called Zaire and is now known as the Democratic Republic of the Congo). He told of a great revival there with thousands of believers being baptized into Christ. After the session, Anna went forward to meet him. She said, "I know there is probably no way you would have known them, but have you ever heard of David and Svea Flood?" The man's eyes filled with tears and he said, "I am the little boy that your mother led to Christ, and in our village, the name of your mother is remembered with honor, for she is the one who led us to the One who gives us eternal life."[14]

In the end, David Flood was caught by the enemy's bait, which became a trap of offense. He became offended with God, and the result was a wasted life cut short by bitterness and resentment. Praise the Lord for his daughter bringing him back to the Lord before he died.

On the other hand, Svea Flood looked into the face of her circumstances with faith and planted her life as a seed for that one little African boy, and "The rest is history," as they say.

I doubt that John thought his ministry would end up this way. And, until now, he was sure who Jesus was—so, what changed?

> *John answered them, saying, "I baptize with water, but there stands One among you whom you do not know. It is He who, coming after me, is preferred*

---

[14] The story of David and Svea Flood and their daughter Anna is written in the book *Fresh Power* by Jim Cymbala.

https://www.mefc.org/content.cfm?id=151&blog. Accessed January 17, 2022.

> *before me, whose sandal strap I am not worthy to loose."*

John 1:26-27 (NKJV)

> *The next day John saw Jesus coming toward him, and said, "Behold! The Lamb of God who takes away the sin of the world! This is He of whom I said, 'After me comes a Man who is preferred before me, for He was before me.' I did not know Him; but that He should be revealed to Israel, therefore I came baptizing with water."*

John 1:29-31 (NKJV)

A Fresh Perspective

Instead of celebrating the ministry of Jesus, John sounds more like a man who is depressed and discouraged.

> *Jesus replied, "Go back and report to John what you hear and see: The blind receive sight, the lame walk, those who have leprosy are cleansed, the deaf hear, the dead are raised, and the good news is proclaimed to the poor Blessed is anyone who does not stumble on account of me."*

Matthew 11:4-6

A fresh perspective starts by understanding two essential truths:

1. It's never been about you, John.

He said it best when he declared.

> *To this John replied, 'A person can receive only what is given them from heaven. You yourselves can testify that I said, 'I am not the Messiah but am sent ahead of him.' The bride belongs to the bridegroom. The friend who attends the bridegroom waits and listens for him, and is full of joy when he hears the bridegroom's*

voice. That joy is mine, and it is now complete. **He must become greater; I must become less**" *[emphasis mine]*

John 3:27-30

2. The real issue is not about your ministry, but what God is doing on the earth.

When God invited us to join Him in the great adventure, where did we come up with the idea that it would be easy? I'm sure you have heard the statement; "The safest place is to be in the center of God's will."

There may be a few folks who might challenge that statement.

- Ask John and see what he says about it. (Matthew 11:1-6).
- Ask Paul and see what he says about it. (2 Corinthians 11:21-29).
- Ask Daniel and see what he says about it. (Daniel 6:1-14).
- Ask Stephen to see what he says about it. (Acts 7:54-60).
- And, especially ask Jesus about it as they were driving spikes into His hands and feet!

Maybe the issue is a better choice of words. Being in the center of God's will is the best place to be, but it may not necessarily be the safest. Especially if your definition of safe is freedom from pain, suffering, and intense pressure.

- Grapes must be crushed to make wine.
- Diamonds form under pressure.
- Olives are pressed to release oil.
- A seed must be broken in order to grow.
- If God is going to work His work in us, we must trust the process.

The Promise He Needed

Jesus replied, "Go back and report to John what you hear and see: The blind receive sight, the lame walk, those who have leprosy are cleansed, the deaf hear, the dead are raised, and the good news is proclaimed to the poor. Blessed is anyone who does not stumble [offended] on account of me."

Matthew 11:4-6

Jesus answered John's question in a strange way: "Blessed is anyone who does not stumble [offended] on account of me."

Why talk about people being healed instead of sending a legion of angels to rescue John? Does Jesus not care what happened to his friend?

You notice that it was when John heard about all the miracles he asked, "Are you the one who is to come, or should we expect someone else?"

Why would the works cause John to doubt? Would it not inspire him? People do not usually say, "if one more person gets healed, I will have a crisis of faith."

John was saying, why are all these good things happening, and I'm still in prison?

Maybe you're not the one; perhaps you are just another faith healer but not really the son of God.

I'm having a crisis over here; all you care about are the people…but, what about me?

Jesus gave a strange response to John's question: "And blessed is he who is not offended because of Me" (Matthew 11:6, NKJV). The statement doesn't seem to fit the context, or does it?

What was Jesus really saying to John? This is your assignment, your path, your purpose. I'm not going to stop the pain; it will short circuit the assignment if I do. Many are offended because Jesus didn't promise them that there would not be a time of pressure, suffering, or pain, and others don't seem to have it at all.

A Final Thought

> *Then He said to the disciples, 'It is impossible that no offenses should come, but woe to him through whom they do come!'*
>
> Luke 17:1 (NKJV)

The Greek word for offend comes from the word, *skandalon*. This word originally referred to, "the part of the trap in someone's way." In the New Testament, it often describes, "an entrapment used by the enemy." Offense is a tool of the devil to being people into captivity. (See 2 Timothy 2:24-26).[15]

The word *offended* means, "to become scandalized!" We think of a scandal as a shocking piece of dirt or gossip about someone we would never consider to be true. What happens when you hear something about someone that is scandalous? It changes your entire view of that person.

No longer do you have the ability to view that person with the same objectivity as before. Your mind is now ensnared or trapped by a prejudicial way of thinking when it comes to that individual. You are always viewing your relationship with that person through a skewed filter by what you perceive to be true.

This is the snare of the enemy for us with the Father. His evil design is to filter our relationship with the Father through the circumstances of life. He wants us to blame the Father for allowing the things that shouldn't have happened or for not doing what we asked Him to do.

---

[15] John Bevere, *The Bait of Satan,* (Orlando, FL: Creation House, 1994; 1997), 3.

Skandalizo is just that. It is a baited trap designed to ensnare you so that you can never again feel, communicate with, or be intimate with the Father the way you once did.

The enemy wants you to become so offended by Father God that you can never see Him, love Him, serve Him, or worship Him the way you once did. Every trap has bait. You and I do not just blindly stumble into being offended by Jesus. The bait of Satan for John is the spirit of offense. This came as a result of feeling betrayed by the Father. John does what the Father told him to do and calls out Herod for marrying his brother's wife. The next thing you know, Herod calls for his head on a silver platter.

John the Baptist's life is hanging in the balance. His entire legacy would be written as one dying for his faith in obedience to the Father or one allowing the spirit of offense to ensnare him with a feeling of betrayal towards the Father.

Which would it be?

In the end, even the wild man John the Baptist needed a little reassurance. Once Jesus reassured Him by signs, wonders, miracles, and His word, John was filled with the faith necessary to die.

The acceptance of the Father is all I need to know who I am and for what purpose I have been called.

For all of us, our heart cry to Jesus in the face of betrayal is just like Philip's in John 14:8 when he's feeling betrayed by the fact that Jesus is going away, "Lord, show us the Father and that will be enough for us." He said the same thing that John the Baptist said in prison, "Are you the Coming One, or do we look for another?"

In the end, John the Baptist, Philip, and all the disciples shook off that feeling of betrayal of the Father. And they willingly gave their lives for His Son and the Gospel.

7

Betrayed by the Fear of Others

Paul's Thorn in the Flesh

Will we look at our weakness as a key to God's power or a stumbling block to our own plans? Are we willing to give up our own strength, accolades, and praise from man because we truly believe Christ is greater? Will we see God's grace and strength even in our suffering?

Christina Patterson[16]

Even if I should choose to boast, I would not be a fool, because I would be speaking the truth. But I refrain, so no one will think more of me than is warranted by what I do or say, or because of these surpassingly great revelations. Therefore, in order to keep me from

---

[16] Christina Patterson, *What Is That "Thorn in the Flesh" and Why Would God Give One to Paul (and Us)?* https://www.ibelieve.com/faith/what-is-that-thorn-in-the-flesh-and-why-would-god-give-one-to-paul-and-us.html Accessed February 12, 2022.

> *becoming conceited, I was given a thorn in my flesh, a messenger of Satan, to torment me. Three times I pleaded with the Lord to take it away from me. But he said to me, "My grace is sufficient for you, for my power is made perfect in weakness. "Therefore I will boast all the more gladly about my weaknesses, so that Christ's power may rest on me. That is why, for Christ's sake, I delight in weaknesses, in insults, in hardships, in persecutions, in difficulties. For when I am weak, then I am strong.*
>
> 2 Corinthians 12:6-10

Paul had a thorn in the flesh; that much is certain. But what is not clear is the source of his thorn. Paul described his thorn in the flesh as "a messenger of Satan sent to torment me," which sounds painful and extremely evil.

Paul's word for thorn is not a little prick in your finger that you received the last time you pruned your rose bushes. Not to say that any splinter in your skin is not painful. But here, the word thorn depicts something used for a stake that people were impaled on to be crucified. Paul's use of that particular word conveyed the seriousness of his situation.

Was it a physical sickness?

John Bloom, writing in, *Why You Have That Thorn*, observed:

Just like Paul's, our thorns weaken us. Sometimes they are visible to others, but often they are hidden from public view, known only to those who know us best. And they are never romantic, never heroic. Rather, they almost always humble us in embarrassing rather than noble ways. They not only seem to impede our effectiveness and fruitfulness, but they also are more likely to detract from rather than enhance our reputations. Which is why we, like Paul, plead with God to remove them (2 Corinthians 12:8).[17]

Many Bible teachers believe that Paul's thorn was some physical ailment—so painful and so pressing that it had the potential to shipwreck his ministry.

The case has been made that Paul's thorn was an eye affliction. Paul indeed lent some weight to that argument when he said in Galatians 6:11, "See what large letters I use as I write to you with my own hand!" Was Paul giving a signal to his physical challenge? Was he going blind, or was he already at the point where someone had to write his letters for him? We don't know; all we can do is speculate—and any good Bible student will tell you it's not wise to guess when the Bible does not give a clear answer.

Or was it something so troubling that Paul didn't want to go into more details than he already did?

From this pastor's viewpoint, I believe that Paul's "thorn in the flesh" was the rejection of the church in Jerusalem. As a case in point, I think one of the reasons Paul didn't sign his name to the book of Hebrews (as its author) was because he was concerned, that they would not read it and heed its wisdom and direction.

Why was there a strain with the church in Jerusalem? How could that relationship impact Paul to the point of despair?

To understand what Paul faced, you have to consider his former resume. He was not one of the original twelve, nor was he numbered with the 120 gathered in the upper room (Acts 1-2). Quite the contrary. While the 120 disciples were being baptized with the power of the Holy

---

[17] John Bloom, *Why You Have That Thorn*,
https://www.desiringgod.org/articles/why-you-have-that-thorn. Accessed February 1, 2022.

Spirit, Paul launched a crusade to stamp out all mention of the name of Jesus Christ.

When he wrote to the church in Philippi, he gave a detailed account of his religious resume. It was impressive.

> *If someone else thinks they have reasons to put confidence in the flesh, I have more: circumcised on the eighth day, of the people of Israel, of the tribe of Benjamin, a Hebrew of Hebrews; in regard to the law, a Pharisee; as for zeal, persecuting the church; as for righteousness based on the law, faultless. But whatever were gains to me I now consider loss for the sake of Christ. What is more, I consider everything a loss because of the surpassing worth of knowing Christ Jesus my Lord, for whose sake I have lost all things. I consider them garbage, that I may gain Christ and be found in him, not having a righteousness of my own that comes from the law, but that which is through faith in Christ—the righteousness that comes from God on the basis of faith. I want to know Christ—yes, to know the power of his resurrection and participation in his sufferings, becoming like him in his death, and so, somehow, attaining to the resurrection from the dead.*
>
> Philippians 3:4-11

Think about that Paul was fast becoming one of the most distinguished Pharisees of his generation. As a young man, he studied at the feet of Gamaliel, the master teacher/rabbi of his day (Acts 22:3). As far as an up-and-coming religious leader, there were no limitations. But then something unexpected happened. One day as he headed to Damascus to find more of this hated sect, he met the Lord Jesus Christ—who turned his world right-side up. He gave up everything to become a member of this new thing called Christianity and preach the Gospel of Christ.

> *Then Saul, still breathing threats and murder against the disciples of the Lord, went to the high priest and asked letters from him to the synagogues of Damascus, so that if he found any who were of the Way, whether men or women, he might bring them bound to Jerusalem. As he journeyed he came near Damascus, and suddenly a light shone around him from heaven. Then he fell to the ground, and heard a voice saying to him, "Saul, Saul, why are you persecuting Me?" And he said, "Who are You, Lord?" Then the Lord said, "I am Jesus, whom you are persecuting. It is hard for you to kick against the goads." So he, trembling and astonished, said, "Lord, what do You want me to do?" Then the Lord said to him, "Arise and go into the city, and you will be told what you must do."*
>
> Acts 9:1-6 (NKJV)

The book of Acts records the reaction of the Church in Jerusalem upon seeing Saul (later Paul) for the first time.

> *When he came to Jerusalem, he tried to join the disciples, but they were all afraid of him, not believing that he really was a disciple.*
>
> Acts 9:26

What a shock it must have been seeing up close and personal the man they all feared. This is the same man involved in the murder of one of the church's early leaders, a man named Stephen.

> *Then they cried out with a loud voice, stopped their ears, and ran at him with one accord; and they cast him out of the city and stoned him.* ***And the witnesses laid down their clothes at the feet of a young man***

> ***named Saul*** *And they stoned Stephen as he was calling on God and saying, "Lord Jesus, receive my spirit." Then he knelt down and cried out with a loud voice, "Lord, do not charge them with this sin." And when he had said this, he fell asleep. Now Saul was consenting to his death.*
>
> Acts 7:57-60; 8:1 (NKJV)

If you want more details about how he felt about his past, read his testimony to his young protégé and son in the faith, Timothy.

> *And I thank Christ Jesus our Lord who has enabled me, because He counted me faithful, putting me into the ministry, although I was formerly a blasphemer, a persecutor, and an insolent man; but I obtained mercy because I did it ignorantly in unbelief.*
>
> 1 Timothy 1:12-13 (NKJV)

- He was a blasphemer denying that Jesus was THE Christ, the Son of God. He spent many days and nights forcing others to deny the same or face imprisonment or death.

- He was a persecutor of the church and used brute force to shut down any mention of the name of Jesus.

- He was an insolent man who disrespected any other religious opinion but his own. He was so zealous for his religion that if you disagreed with him, he would kill you—in the name of the Lord, of course.

Paul was not ashamed to admit acting "ignorantly in unbelief." As stated earlier, Paul was considered one of the most brilliant religious minds of his day, and yet, he was blinded to the truth of the gospel. (See 2 Corinthians 4:3-4, NKJV). On the road to Damascus, he discovered that his persecution was not only directed at the church in Jerusalem, but he was actually persecuting Christ.

> *And he said, "Who are You, Lord?" Then the Lord said, "I am Jesus, whom you are persecuting. It is hard for you to kick against the goads"*
>
> Acts 9:5 (NKJV)

So, it's understandable that the church in Jerusalem thought he was trying to convince them of his conversion for sinister reasons. Considering the horrible things this religious zealot had done, how were they supposed to believe he had a change of heart?

In fact, he didn't have a change of heart...HE HAD A NEW HEART! Paul was now a living embodiment of what he wrote to the church at Corinth.

> *Therefore, if anyone is in Christ, he is a new creation; old things have passed away; behold, all things have become new.*
>
> 2 Corinthians 5:17 (NKJV)

There was nothing he could say or do to ever endear himself to the church in Jerusalem and most of the Apostles. If it had not been for Barnabas, Paul would have never been able to set foot anywhere near the church.

> *But Barnabas took him and brought him to the apostles. He told them how Saul on his journey had seen the Lord and that the Lord had spoken to him, and how in Damascus he had preached fearlessly in the name of Jesus.*
>
> Acts 9:27

It became clear that he and Peter didn't get along very well. You don't have to read between the lines about their relationship. You can see the confrontation in the book of Galatians as their differences exploded into a virtual war of words. Paul was not shy about calling out the man most considered the lead, or chief, apostle.

When Cephas came to Antioch, I opposed him to his face, because he stood condemned. For before certain men came from James, he used to eat with the Gentiles. But when they arrived, he began to draw back and separate himself from the Gentiles because he was afraid of those who belonged to the circumcision group. The other Jews joined him in his hypocrisy, so that by their hypocrisy even Barnabas was led astray.

Galatians 2:11-13

There was jealousy among the other Apostles toward Paul as well. After all, he was late to the party. He hadn't walked with Jesus the way they had. He had not been there when Jesus fed over 5,000, raised Lazarus from the dead, and any number of other miracles. He hadn't endured the threat of losing his life after the crucifixion the way they did.

Paul was indeed the victim of betrayal at the hands of his peers because they could never get past their fears and struggles.

Fear is the absence of faith. Corrie Ten Boom said, "Worry is a cycle of inefficient thoughts whirling around a center of fear." I agree—fear and faith cannot coexist.

The spirit of fear has a cycle as follows:

- Fear is caused by doubt.
- Insecurity creates doubt.
- Insecurity is the result of a lack of identity.
- A lack of identity is the result of rejection.

I believe it is evident that the church in Jerusalem projected rejection upon Paul due to their insecurities.

To make matters worse, Paul continually suffered betrayal at the hands of spiritual sons and those he was discipling. He writes:

> *This you know, that all those in Asia have turned away from me, among whom are Phygellus and Hermogenes.*
>
> 2 Timothy 1:15 (NKJV)

We have no details as to who these two men were. It is a common belief that they were leaders, and teachers, in the church who stood against Paul and refused to defend him in Rome.

Paul had poured his life into the Asian believers, and when he needed them the most, they turned away from him. They were ashamed to be associated with his ministry. Think about that. A portion of his life's work in the Kingdom is no more. Paul poured his life into spiritual sons, and now in an instant, they are gone.

> *Be diligent to come to me quickly; for Demas has forsaken me, having loved this present world, and has departed for Thessalonica—Crescens for Galatia, Titus for Dalmatia. Only Luke is with me. Get Mark and bring him with you, for he is useful to me for ministry. And Tychicus I have sent to Ephesus. Bring the cloak that I left with Carpus at Troas when you come—and the books, especially the parchments. Alexander the coppersmith did me much harm. May the Lord repay him according to his works. You also must beware of him, for he has greatly resisted our words. At my first defense, no one stood with me, but all forsook me. May it not be charged against them.*
>
> 2 Timothy 4:9-16 (NKJV)

Some of the most disappointing things I have ever witnessed were when I watched spiritual sons steal ministries from spiritual fathers who had put their trust and faith in them. It's repulsive and heartbreaking. I have seen the most ruthless behavior in the name of *doing God's will* in ministry. I have watched men steal ministries from leaders that were dying. I witnessed sons split their own biological

Betrayal

father's church and take it to begin their own ministry. I have seen spiritual fathers hand over ministries to spiritual sons to see them immediately remove any and every source of that spiritual father's identity and legacy from the church. I have watched as lifelong ministry friends and staff of more than three decades smell blood in the water, so to speak, in a man's life and attempt to steal his life's work in ministry for themselves, all in the name of doing what's moral, ethical, and right in the sight of God. People like that use the hypocritical moral high ground of the idea that *we are trying to save your ministry*. To which I say "hogwash." They do it for greed and self-gain.

Yes, Paul also knew the pain of betrayal all too well. From Demas who had forsaken him, "having loved this present world," (2 Timothy 4:10, NKJV); to the accusations of those in Corinth about money. They indicated that Paul was a burden to them. Paul wrote the entire letter of 2 Corinthians defending himself to the church, telling them in 2 Corinthians 12:14 NKJV, "for I do not seek yours, but you." Who do they think they are questioning? Someone with the track record and pedigree of the Apostle Paul doesn't owe them an explanation about anything.

I have seen it with my own eyes. I have lived it in my own life. You spend your entire life serving God and others to have some immature, wet-behind-the-ears church member or staff member question your every decision. Well, I guess if Paul had to deal with it, who are we to complain? And, in dealing with it, he remained humble and kind as he writes.

> *For we are glad when we are weak and you are strong. And, this also we pray, that you may be made complete.*
>
> 2 Corinthians 13:9 (NKJV)

Yes, I must say the ministry isn't for sissies. You will have to love those who hate you, despise you and use you for their own sake. But isn't that what Jesus told us to expect? Yes, but He said that of the world. I didn't know it would be in the church and ministry also. As a matter of fact, the world has always treated me better than the church. It makes you wonder what that says about who is really a part of the church?

A Final Thought

What is the lesson we are to learn from Paul's thorn? When you are actively involved in ministry, you can be sure that the enemy will send a "thorn," a "messenger of Satan," to stop you. Whether it's through the betrayal of spiritual sons, the rejection of an entire church, or a physical malady—the enemy will do all in his power to shut you down.

Author and Bible teacher Warren W. Wiersbe observed:

> As Paul prayed about his problem, God gave him a deeper insight into what He was doing. Paul learned that his thorn in the flesh was a gift from God. What a strange gift! There was only one thing for Paul to do: accept the gift from God and allow God to accomplish His purposes. God wanted to keep Paul from being "exalted above measure," and this was His way of accomplishing it.[18]

We may feel betrayed, rejected, or cast aside like yesterday's news, but the bottom line is in the midst of whatever the enemy throws at us, God's grace is sufficient...sufficient for what you ask? For whatever we face!

> *Concerning this thing I pleaded with the Lord three times that it might depart from me. And He said to me,* ***"My grace is sufficient for you, for My strength is made perfect in weakness."*** *Therefore most gladly I will rather boast in my infirmities, that the power of*

---

[18] Warren W. Wiersbe, *Be Encouraged,* (Wheaton, IL: Victor Books, 1988). 139.

Betrayal

Christ may rest upon me. Therefore I take pleasure in infirmities, in reproaches, in needs, in persecutions, in distresses, for Christ's sake. For when I am weak, then I am strong.

2 Corinthians 12:8-10 (NKJV)

8

The Anatomy of a Betrayer

Judas—The Ultimate Betrayal

> For you will certainly carry out God's purpose, however you act, but it makes a difference to you whether you serve like Judas or like John.
>
> C.S. Lewis, *The Problem of Pain*

> *Then one of the Twelve—the one called Judas Iscariot—went to the chief priests and asked, "What are you willing to give me if I deliver him over to you?" So they counted out for him thirty pieces of silver. From then on Judas watched for an opportunity to hand him over.*
>
> Matthew 26:14-16

Throughout history, certain names have evoked an immediate reaction; names such as Hitler, Stalin, Oswald, John Wilkes Booth, Benedict Arnold, and Osama bin Laden are a few of the most recognized. Watching their insidious deeds in a history channel documentary, or reading about them in a book, reminds us of the darkness of the human heart.

In my estimation, there is one name that stands above the rest. It is a name that is synonymous with the ultimate act of evil—his name is Judas Iscariot.

Whether you are a Bible teacher or a person with no religious inclination, you know the name and what it stands for—treachery and betrayal. Bible teacher Mark Adams said, "It is little wonder then, that today men name their sons after Paul, and their dogs after Nero but the only thing named after Judas is the stockyard animal that guides the others into the slaughterhouse."[19]

To better understand one of the most hated men in human history, it might be helpful to ask a few questions:

Who Was This Man Named Judas Iscariot?

Reading through the scriptures we can ascertain some insight into his life. His betrayal is recounted in all four gospel accounts [Matthew 26, 27; Mark 14; Luke 22; John 12,13, 18]. It would appear at the outset of his calling (to follow Jesus) that there wasn't much in his background that would suggest that he would eventually betray Jesus. It's also true that many who have their names etched in the pages of history (as betrayers) didn't appear to be so at first.

Betrayers usually start with an agenda that unfolds over time and is known only to them. If you scratch the surface of their actions, you will find a feigned loyalty to the cause until their real motives are revealed.

1. He came from a different part of the country than the rest of the apostles.

His surname, Iscariot, is an identifier that gives us a hint of where he was born and raised. Of all the men called by Jesus, it appears that Judas Iscariot is the only one whose birthplace is listed. Robert Cargill,

---

[19] https://www.redlandbaptist.net/sermon/judas-iscariot-an-betrayer-or-betrayaccessed. accessed March 10, 2022.

assistant professor of classics and religious studies at the University of Iowa said, "Some scholars have linked his surname *Iscariot* to Queriot (or Kerioth), a town located south of Jerusalem in Judea. One of the things that might set Judas apart from the rest of Jesus's disciples is that Judas is not from Galilee. Jesus is from the northern part of Israel or Roman Palestine. But Judas's surname might be evidence that he's from the southern part of the country, meaning he may be a little bit of an outsider."[20]

2. His name reflects his upbringing.

Judas was a popular name. Many Jewish parents chose that name to honor a man named Judas Maccabeus, who led a war for Jewish independence in 164 B.C. One of Jesus' half-brothers was named Judas or Jude. It's also true that there was another apostle of Jesus named Judas. He was referred to as Judas, son of James, but to distinguish one from the other, he went by the name, some say nickname, of Thaddaeus.

There is no reason to believe that Judas came from anything other than a loving home, with parents who did all they could to bring Judas up in a caring environment. Like all good Jewish parents, they chose a name that would indicate their belief that their son Judas would live a blessed life. Little did they know what was ahead.

3. He was part of the apostolic team.

Judas did not fill out an application to become a member of the apostolic team—Christ himself called him. (See Mark 3:13-19). And, with his calling, he would have been included in the very foundation of the Church—not a small thing to consider.

---

[20] https://www.history.com/news/why-judas-betrayed-jesus. accessed March 10, 2022.

Betrayal

Three Old Testament prophecies point to the fact that Jesus already knew who Judas really was, and He was not taken by surprise by anything that happened. (See John 6:70; Acts 2:23).

Even my close friend, someone I trusted, one who shared my bread, has turned against me.

Psalm 41:9

If an enemy were insulting me, I could endure it; if a foe were rising against me, I could hide. But it is you, a man like myself, my companion, my close friend, with whom I once enjoyed sweet fellowship at the house of God, as we walked about among the worshipers.

Psalm 55:12-14

I told them, 'If you think it best, give me my pay; but if not, keep it.' So they paid me thirty pieces of silver. And the Lord said to me, 'Throw it to the potter'—the handsome price at which they valued me! So I took the thirty pieces of silver and threw them to the potter at the house of the Lord.

Zechariah 11:12-13

If you saw the apostolic team ministering in the villages (see Mark 6:6-13), you would not have picked out Judas and said, "There is the traitor!" There were no outward signs that this man would commit an act of betrayal so grievous that his name would live in infamy.

For over three years, Judas saw the ministry of Jesus from the inside. He not only heard the teachings of Christ, but he had the privilege of walking and talking with the son of God. And yet, in all of those experiences, he never gave his heart entirely to Christ. His commitment to sharing the gospel of the Kingdom only went as far as his self-interest. When it was no longer a viable option to accomplish his goal—more on why he did what he did later—he opened himself up to the control of Satan.

The Anatomy of a Betrayer

Author and Bible teacher Colin Smith writes:

He directly witnessed the miracles. When Jesus fed the 5,000, Judas was there. He took the bread and distributed it along with the other disciples. When Jesus calmed the storm, Judas was there. And he was there when Jesus raised Lazarus from the dead. You can't have better evidence for faith than Judas had. Judas heard all the teaching of Jesus, too. He heard the Sermon on the Mount, so he knew there is a narrow road that leads to life and a broad road that leads to destruction. He heard the warnings Jesus spoke to the Pharisees, so he knew there is a hell to shun and a heaven to gain. He heard the parable of the prodigal son, so he knew God is ready to welcome and forgive those who have wasted themselves in many sins.

With Judas's own eyes, he saw the clearest evidence. With his own ears, he heard the finest teaching. With his own feet, he followed the greatest example. And yet this man still betrayed Jesus."[21]

4. He was trusted to oversee the treasury.

> *Six days before the Passover, Jesus came to Bethany, where Lazarus lived, whom Jesus had raised from the dead. Here a dinner was given in Jesus' honor. Martha served, while Lazarus was among those reclining at the table with him. Then Mary took about a pint of pure nard, an expensive perfume; she poured it on Jesus' feet and wiped his feet with her hair. And the house was filled with the fragrance of the perfume.*

---

[21] Colin Smith, *4 Things We Can Learn from Judas*, https://www.thegospelcoalition.org/article/4-things-learn-judas/ accessed March 11, 2022.

Betrayal

> *But one of his disciples, Judas Iscariot, who was later to betray him, objected, "Why wasn't this perfume sold and the money given to the poor? It was worth a year's wages" He did not say this because he cared about the poor but because he was a thief;* <u>*as keeper of the money bag, he used to help himself to what was put into it.*</u>
>
> *"Leave her alone," Jesus replied. "It was intended that she should save this perfume for the day of my burial. You will always have the poor among you, but you will not always have me."*
>
> John 12:1-8

When John said, "as keeper of the money bag, he used to help himself to what was put into it," he was writing after the fact, not before. Yes, John said Judas was a thief, but when these events were unfolding, no one, including John, had a clue. You would never choose a person to watch over the finances (of any organization) who was a known thief. That's like asking the fox to oversee the management of the hen house. On the contrary, you choose someone of good character and whose integrity is beyond question. But his true nature was beginning to be revealed as the exchange in John 12 shows.

Why Did Judas Betray Jesus?

It may be an oversimplification to say the devil made him do it (and not inquire further), when before "Satan entered into him" (John 13:27). There were other indications that Judas was headed down the road to betray Jesus.

The story of Judas proves that you can have the best upbringing, mentors and teachers, and open doors to achieve greatness, and still make wrong choices and bad decisions that negate everything good in your life. Luke 22:4 NKJV says, "So he went his way." That one statement sums up this man's life, and it indicates that in the end, Judas decided to go in a different direction, both physically and spiritually.

Below are three possible explanations for why Judas committed such as heinous act.

1. Was it the love of money?

In the first recorded words of Judas, he made critical remarks about Mary wasting money on such extravagance. (See John 12:1-8). It was a show—but it didn't fool Jesus. Judas didn't care about Mary or the poor. He cared about one person—himself. Many Bible teachers believe that Judas had already made up his mind to betray Jesus, and he wanted to take all the money he could before it was too late. Either way, his deception, thievery, and betrayal would soon be exposed for the world to see.

Yes, John did tell us that Judas had taken money from the bag. Maybe Judas felt the other disciples didn't appreciate his hard work or that they should have offered to pay him a little something for his efforts. Taking a few coins out of the money bag could have been justified in a thousand different ways—all of them wrong.

We have no idea how much he took, but it was not his to take, whatever the amount was. In his final act of greed, Judas went to the religious authorities and offered up Jesus for 30 pieces of silver.

> *Then one of the Twelve—the one called Judas Iscariot—went to the chief priests and asked, "What are you willing to give me if I deliver him over to you?" So they counted out for him thirty pieces of silver. From then on Judas watched for an opportunity to hand him over.*
>
> Matthew 26:14-16

Bible teacher Ivor Powell wrote:

The agreed price of betrayal was thirty pieces' silver; the price of a slave. Our finite minds cannot comprehend this act of stupidity. He who dispensed healing to the nation; He who had turned night to day and storms to calm, was valued at the price of a slave in the market place.[22]

2. Was it jealousy?

As stated earlier, Judas was from a town in southern Judea which could have caused him to feel like the odd-man-out among the other disciples.

> It is interesting to note that in every list that names the disciples, Judas Iscariot is always named last. This illustrates the wide gulf that separated Judas from the Lord Jesus Christ. He was isolated from the rest of the disciples because of his background. He was also separated from them spiritually. He was the only unbeliever in the crowd![23]

Becoming jealous, especially in ministry, can lead to disastrous decisions. It is not uncommon for staff members to feel that their ideas for the future of the ministry are better than the one leading. I have seen with my own eyes how team members behave when they sense that their opinions are not as valued as others on the team. Feeling underappreciated and ignored can often lead to circumstances that can derail an otherwise successful ministry.

Is it possible that Judas looked around when some of the most important events were taking place and noticed that only Peter, James, and John were allowed to spend those intimate moments with Jesus? A feeling of being left out could cause one to never be satisfied with their part of the ministry team. It is tragic when team members don't get what they want and would rather rip the team apart and betray their

---

[22] Ivor Powell, Luke's Thrilling Gospel, (Grand Rapids, MI: Kregel Publications, 1965-1984). 444, 445.

[23] https://www.sermonnotebook.org/mark/Mark%2069%20-%20Mark%2014_10-11.htm. accessed March 11, 2022.

leader than deal with the simmering frustrations that lurk underneath the surface.

> 3. Did Judas become disillusioned because Jesus talked about the cross and not overthrowing the Roman yoke?

Did Judas become so disillusioned with the direction of the ministry that he was willing to cast his lot with the Pharisees? It is a widely held belief that Judas was expecting Jesus to somehow lead an insurrection and overthrow the yoke of Roman bondage and restore the nation of Israel to its rightful place in history. Is any of that true? We don't know for sure, and it's safe to say we will never have all the answers.

What we do know for sure is that as Jesus approached the cross, the opposition became stronger. None of this (opposition) escaped the attention of Judas. What Judas had hoped for was not going to happen, and his dream of conquest was dying.

I believe the turning point came when Jesus fed the 5,000 in John 6:1-12. After the miracle of the loaves and fishes, Jesus perceived that the people wanted to come and make him king.

> *After the people saw the sign Jesus performed, they began to say, 'Surely this is the Prophet who is to come into the world.' Jesus, knowing that they intended to come and make him king by force, withdrew again to a mountain by himself Jesus would have no part of it and withdrew from the crowd.*
>
> John 6:14-15

Later in the chapter, Jesus began to talk about eating his flesh and drinking his blood, which was symbolic of total commitment.

> *Jesus said to them, 'Very truly I tell you, unless you eat the flesh of the Son of Man and drink his blood, you have no life in you. Whoever eats my flesh and drinks my blood has eternal life, and I will raise them up at*

> *the last day. For my flesh is real food and my blood is real drink. Whoever eats my flesh and drinks my blood remains in me, and I in them.'*
>
> John 6:53-56

When the disciples heard that they responded in verse 60, "This is a hard teaching. Who can accept it?" And verse 66 states, "From this time many of his disciples turned back and no longer followed him."

When Jesus noticed that many of his fair-weather disciples were walking away, He turned to the Twelve and said in verse 67, "You do not want to leave too, do you?"

Peter speaks for the rest.

> *Lord, to whom shall we go? You have the words of eternal life. We have come to believe and to know that you are the Holy One of God.*
>
> John 6:68-69

Jesus then makes an astonishing statement.

> *Have I not chosen you, the Twelve? Yet one of you is a devil!' (He meant Judas, the son of Simon Iscariot, who, though one of the Twelve, was later to betray him).*
>
> John 6:70-71

This event might have convinced Judas that Jesus was going to be on a cross and not a throne and it was time to take action to try and save himself.

What Can We Learn?

Whether it was greed, jealousy, or disillusionment, we may never know all of the reasons why Judas did what he did. But the fact remains no one suspected that Judas would be the one to betray Jesus. In John 13:21, Jesus announced that, "Very truly I tell you, one of you is going to betray me," and not one of the disciples turned around and pointed their finger at Judas. They had no clue who it might be, which caused Peter to prompt John to write in verse 24, "Ask him (Jesus) which one he means." It was only in answer to that question did Jesus identify the man who will live on in infamy as the man who kissed the door of heaven and went to hell.

> *Jesus answered, "It is the one to whom I will give this piece of bread when I have dipped it in the dish." Then, dipping the piece of bread, he gave it to Judas, the son of Simon Iscariot. As soon as Judas took the bread, Satan entered into him.*
>
> John 13:26-27

1. We can learn that it's possible to be close to Jesus and still have a heart that is hardened by sin.

Some people believe that as long as you go to church, sing the hymns, and do the religious *stuff,* it will be enough to enter heaven. Getting close to Jesus is not the same as knowing Him in a personal relationship. Jesus said in Matthew 7:21-23:

> *Not everyone who says to me, 'Lord, Lord,' will enter the kingdom of heaven, but only the one who does the will of my Father who is in heaven. Many will say to me on that day, 'Lord, Lord, did we not prophesy in your name and in your name drive out demons and in your name perform many miracles?' Then I will tell them plainly, 'I never knew you. Away from me, you evildoers!'*

2. We can learn that there is forgiveness even for the most horrible sin—if we are willing to repent and allow the blood of Jesus to cleanse us.

The Bible records that two disciples betrayed Jesus.

Judas' betrayal was because his heart was never fully committed to the Son of God, and he allowed greed to overtake him.

But there was another disciple, and his name was Peter.

Peter heard the teachings and saw the miracles, just as Judas did. On that fateful night of the Passover, both men made a life-altering decision—one to betray for money and one who denied knowing Him.

But that is where the difference ends. The outcomes were the opposite.

Judas died without a savior. He had remorse but not repentance. The Bible records the following.

> *When Judas, who had betrayed him, saw that Jesus was condemned, he was seized with remorse and returned the thirty pieces of silver to the chief priests and the elders. "I have sinned," he said, "for I have betrayed innocent blood." "What is that to us?" they replied. "That's your responsibility." So Judas threw the money into the temple and left. Then he went away and hanged himself*
>
> Matthew 27:3-5

Peter repented of his denial and received forgiveness. (See Luke 22:61-62; John 21:15-19). He became a foundation stone of the early church.

A Final Thought

Judas chose to betray the son of God. To use modern-day slang: *no one held a gun to his head.* He opened the door to Satan and allowed the enemy to use his greed, jealousy, and disillusionment to drive him into the arms of Christ's enemies. Despite all that Judas contemplated (and all he did), Jesus still gave him an opportunity to repent.

Think about this for a second.

Jesus knew.

He goes into that room with His disciples. He knows He is going to be betrayed. He knows it is Judas who will turn against him. He knows that He has been sold out for a handful of silver. He was stabbed in the back by one He has poured His life into.

Yet, in that room, hours before the death of Jesus, Judas ate too. Jesus fed Judas too. Jesus prayed for Judas too. Jesus washed Judas' feet too. I struggle to fathom that kind of love. A love that would feed the mouth that deceived you. A love that would wash the treasonous feet of the traitor. A love that could forgive even the vilest of betrayals.

I honestly struggle to comprehend it. And then, suddenly, I realize that I'm Judas. And in that moment, I'm so thankful and altogether overwhelmed that Judas ate too.

9

Looks Can Be Deceiving

Joshua Betrayed by the Gibeonites

As we appropriate the life of Christ for moment-by-moment victory, Satan will do everything he can to thwart God's purpose through us. Even though Satan's power is broken, he is not idle.

Theodore H. Epp

The Israelites sampled their provisions but did not inquire of the Lord. Then Joshua made a treaty of peace with them to let them live, and the leaders of the assembly ratified it by oath.

Joshua 9:14-15

When you read Joshua chapter seven, you will see how Joshua's army suffered a crushing defeat at what should have been an easy victory in the small city of Ai. It is easy to see the problem if you read the complete account. Joshua failed to seek God's counsel, and his failure led to presumption and an over-confidence in their power and strength to defeat a relatively insignificant enemy.

Betrayal

> *When they returned to Joshua, they said, "Not all the army will have to go up against Ai. Send two or three thousand men to take it and do not weary the whole army, for only a few people live there." So about three thousand went up; but they were routed by the men of Ai, who killed about thirty-six of them. They chased the Israelites from the city gate as far as the stone quarries and struck them down on the slopes. At this the hearts of the people melted in fear and became like water.*
>
> Joshua 7:3-5

What should have been an overwhelming victory turned out to be a total and complete embarrassment for Joshua and his army. Men died, and the enemy rejoiced, all because of a failure to pray. But, you say, *Joshua did pray*. Yes, but only after his army was routed—not before. Had he prayed beforehand, God would have revealed to him that there was "sin in the camp, and it must be dealt with before moving forward." As the old-time preachers used to say, "If you pray in time of victory, you will never have to plead in time of defeat." As Joshua prayed, cried, and begged God to forgive him for the defeat, the following happened.

> *The Lord said to Joshua, "Stand up! What are you doing down on your face? Israel has sinned; they have violated my covenant, which I commanded them to keep. They have taken some of the devoted things; they have stolen, they have lied, they have put them with their own possessions. That is why the Israelites cannot stand against their enemies; they turn their backs and run because they have been made liable to destruction. I will not be with you anymore unless you destroy whatever among you is devoted to destruction.*
>
> Joshua 7:10-12

The result of Joshua's prayer was that God revealed the sin of Achan, and judgment was meted out. (See Joshua 7:14-26). The army could not move forward in victory until Joshua exposed the sin, as harsh as it seemed.

As Joshua chapter nine opens, you would have thought Joshua had learned his lesson. I'm sure he thought, I will never again fail to consult the Lord again.

But a mere two chapters later, we find history repeating itself.

The Gibeonites show up—and here we go again!

Joshua learned (the hard way) that failure to seek God's wisdom will lead you down a road you don't want to go.

There are two major lessons we need to learn from this story.

The Enemy Is Very Subtle

As the chapter opens, the Canaanite kings band together to fight against Joshua.

> *Now when all the kings west of the Jordan heard about these things—the kings in the hill country, in the western foothills, and along the entire coast of the Mediterranean Sea as far as Lebanon (the kings of the Hittites, Amorites, Canaanites, Perizzites, Hivites and Jebusites)—they came together to wage war against Joshua and Israel"*

Joshua 9:1-2

To see these kings, who were once rivals, joining together against a common enemy (Israel), reminds me of the saying, "The enemy of my enemy is my friend."

Enter the Gibeonites.

They figured there was no way they could stand up against the army of Joshua. They decided to go in another direction—why fight and die when they could use deception to get their way.

Betrayal

The Gibeonites arrived on the scene with one objective—to trick Joshua into allying with them—and it worked.

1. The plan was clever.

   However, when the people of Gibeon heard what Joshua had done to Jericho and Ai, they resorted to a ruse: They went as a delegation whose donkeys were loaded with worn-out sacks and old wineskins, cracked and mended. They put worn and patched sandals on their feet and wore old clothes. All the bread of their food supply was dry and moldy. Then they went to Joshua in the camp at Gilgal and said to him and the Israelites, "We have come from a distant country; make a treaty with us." The Israelites said to the Hivites, "But perhaps you live near us, so how can we make a treaty with you?"

   "We are your servants," they said to Joshua.

   But Joshua asked, "Who are you and where do you come from?"

   They answered: "Your servants have come from a very distant country because of the fame of the Lord your God. For we have heard reports of him. all that he did in Egypt, and all that he did to the two kings of the Amorites east of the Jordan—Sihon king of Heshbon, and Og king of Bashan, who reigned in Ashtaroth. And our elders and all those living in our country said to us, 'Take provisions for your journey; go and meet them and say to them, "We are your servants; make a treaty with us." 'This bread of ours was warm when we packed it at home on the day we left to come to you. But now see how dry and moldy it is. And these wineskins that we filled were new, but see how cracked

Looks Can Be Deceiving

> *they are. And our clothes and sandals are worn out by the very long journey."*
>
> *The Israelites sampled their provisions but did not inquire of the Lord. Then Joshua made a treaty of peace with them to let them live, and the leaders of the assembly ratified it by oath.*
>
> Joshua 9:3-14

How did they pull it off?

- They made Joshua believe they traveled from a great distance and assured him that they fully believed in the God of the Israelites. "We're on your side," they said.

- They told Joshua they had heard about all the powerful things God had done for them as they journeyed through the wilderness.

- They said they were from an area over which Joshua had no authority and a place where God had given no specific commandment.

- They were wearing dirty clothes and shoes, worn out and falling apart.

- The donkeys were loaded down with old wineskins that were made to look cracked and mended.

- The bread they were carrying was dry and moldy.

Everything they did was an act of deception to fool Joshua and the leadership that they posed no threat—and to pretend that they needed to be protected.

2. The problem was obvious.

God had told Joshua not to make any alliances with non-Israelites—period. God told Joshua to destroy (wipe out) all the Canaanites. Deuteronomy 20:17-18 plainly states:

> *But you shall utterly destroy them, the Hittite, the Amorite, the Canaanite, the Perizzite, the Hivite and the Jebusite, just as the Lord your God has commanded you, so that they will not teach you to act in accordance with all the detestable practices which they have done [in worship and service] for their gods, and in this way cause you to sin against the Lord your God.*

The problem lies in the fact that instead of following God's instructions, Joshua believed the Gibeonites and made a treaty: "Then Joshua made a treaty of peace with them to let them live, and the leaders of the assembly ratified it by oath."

Bible teacher and author Alan Redpath observed:

So what does Satan do? He speaks to us concerning possible alliances that appear to be very trifling compared to our devotion to the Lord Jesus Christ. He speaks to us about a certain part of our lives over which he suggests the Lord Jesus Christ has no authority and concerning which Christ has given us no command, which is, as it were, so much on the circumference that it really will not matter anyway if we listen to the devil. He challenges us on the necessity for entire, thorough consecration."[24]

Redpath says that the enemy will do everything to move us away from the high standard required to follow the Lord Jesus Christ fully. If the devil can move us into an area of compromise, even in the minor things, his job of deception can continue to operate.

We Must Become More Strategic

Joshua fell right into their hands. Instead of asking the Lord to reveal any deception, he decided based on his own wisdom.

---

[24] Alan Redpath, *Victorious Christian Living*, (Grand Rapids, MI: Fleming H. Revell Company, 1955). 139.

> *So the men [of Israel] took some of their own provisions [and offered them in friendship], and [foolishly] <u>did not ask for the counsel of the Lord,</u> (emphasis mine). Joshua made peace with them and made a covenant (treaty) with them, to let them live; and the leaders of the congregation [of Israel] swore an oath to them. (emphasis mine).*
>
> Joshua 9:14-15 AMP

That one statement says it all: "and [foolishly] did not ask for the counsel of the Lord."

Failure to access God's wisdom is caused by two things.

1. <u>Presumption</u>

One standard definition of presumption is an "idea that is taken to be true, and often used as the basis for other ideas, although it is not known for certain."[25]

The Bible is filled with instances where people acted on an assumption (another way of saying presumption) without God's wisdom or permission.

- Leviticus 10:1-2

   Aaron's sons Nadab and Abihu took their censers, put fire in them and added incense; and they offered unauthorized fire before the Lord, contrary to his command. So fire came out from the presence of the Lord and consumed them, and they died before the Lord.

---

[25] https://www.merriam-webster.com/dictionary/presumption#synonyms. accessed March 20, 2022.

- 2 Samuel 6:6-7

   When they came to the threshing floor of Nakon, Uzzah reached out and took hold of the ark of God, because the oxen stumbled. The Lord's anger burned against Uzzah because of his irreverent act; therefore God struck him down, and he died there beside the ark of God.

- James 4:13-17

   Now listen, you who say, 'Today or tomorrow we will go to this or that city, spend a year there, carry on business and make money.' Why, you do not even know what will happen tomorrow. What is your life? You are a mist that appears for a little while and then vanishes. Instead, you ought to say, 'If it is the Lord's will, we will live and do this or that.' As it is, you boast in your arrogant schemes. All such boasting is evil. If anyone, then, knows the good they ought to do and doesn't do it, it is sin for them.

How foolish are we when faced with issues that we do not ask for God's wisdom? The Bible teaches that as Christians, we can rely on God's wisdom and not try to figure things out on our own.

> *If any of you lacks wisdom [to guide him through a decision or circumstance], he is to ask of [our benevolent] God, who gives to everyone generously and without rebuke or blame, and it will be given to him.*
>
> James 1:5 (AMP)
>
> *It is because of him that you are in Christ Jesus, who has become for us wisdom from God—that is, our righteousness, holiness, and redemption.*
>
> 1 Corinthians 1:30

Presumption often creeps in when we think that the situation is something that we can handle without God's help. It's the *why bother God with this, when I am capable of making the right decision* syndrome. More often than not, we go back to beg God to fix whatever mess we've made.

I've learned that decisions made under pressure will often lead to disastrous consequences. Joshua made a hasty decision and was betrayed by the Gibeonites.

Theodore Epp wrote, "Be especially careful of decisions that have to be made under pressure." He continued, "I have found it wise to stand and wait. God will never let an opportunity go by that He wants us to have. Even if we are late, and it is God's desire for us to have what He has planned, we will receive it."[26]

I believe the Psalmist prayer should be our daily prayer:

> *Keep back Your servant also from presumptuous sins;*
> *Let them not have dominion over me.*
> *Then I shall be blameless,*
> *And I shall be innocent of great transgression.*
>
> Psalm 19:13 NKJV

2. <u>Prayerlessness</u>

Joshua's trouble could have been avoided had he prayed before allying with the Gibeonites.

> *So the men [of Israel] took some of their own provisions [and offered them in friendship], and [foolishly] did not ask for the counsel of the Lord.*
>
> Joshua 9:14 (AMP)

---

[26] Theodore H. Epp, *Joshua-Victorious by Faith*, (Lincoln, NE, The Good News Broadcasting Assoc., Inc., 1968). 212.

You can be assured that failure to pray will always lead to problems, rendering the spirit of discernment ineffective.

P.T. Forsythe once said:

The worst sin is prayerlessness. We usually think of murder, adultery, or theft as among the worst. But the root of all sin is self-sufficiency and independence from God. When we fail to wait prayerfully for God's guidance and strength, we are saying, with our actions if not our lips, that we do not need Him. How much of our service is characterized by 'going it alone?'[27]

Many heartbreaking stories tell us how we allowed someone into our circle of influence to find out later we were betrayed. I'm not suggesting we won't ever be fooled by smooth-sounding words or feigned loyalty to our vision. Still, there have been many occasions where betrayal could have been avoided if only prayer was a central theme in the decision-making process.

The prophet Samuel was asked to pray for the people after they realized they had made a mistake asking God for a king. Samuel declared that it would be a sin against the Lord if he should fail to pray for them.

> *As for me, far be it from me that I should sin against the Lord by failing to pray for you. And I will teach you the way that is good and right.*
>
> 1 Samuel 12:23

What an amazing statement.

Yes, prayer is that important and cannot and must not be neglected. Prayer is more than a suggestion; it is a command. Bible teacher Dave Butts said, "Jesus told His disciples to pray and not give

---

[27] https://gracequotes.org/quote/p-t-forsyth-once-said-the-worst-sin-is-prayerlessness/ accessed March 20, 2022.

up" (see Luke 18:1-8). Paul commanded us to "pray continually" (1 Thessalonians 5:17). Peter wrote that we are to be self-controlled so that we can pray (see 1 Peter 4:7). James commanded us to, "pray for each other" (James 5:16). If failing to do something we are commanded to do is sin, then prayerlessness is surely a major sin for believers."[28]

A Final Thought

Joshua's response to the deception of the Gibeonites is very telling. "Then Joshua made a treaty of peace with them to let them live, and the leaders of the assembly ratified it by oath" (Joshua 9:15*)*. When Joshua allied with the Gibeonites, God held him to his word—he was not allowed to kill them. The mistake was made, and they would have to live with the consequences. They did something God not them not to do. Every time they looked at the Gibeonites, they were reminded of their failure to pray and seek God's counsel.

The mistakes that Joshua made are not unfamiliar to us. Failure to pray can lead us into some of the same alliances that will come back and haunt us for years to come. Proverbs tells us the best way to live.

> *Trust in the Lord with all your heart and lean not on your own understanding; in all your ways submit to him, and he will make your paths straight.*
>
> Proverbs 3:5-6

Despite what the enemy tried to do, look at the outcome.

> *Let them live but let them be woodcutters and water carriers in the service of the whole assembly. So the leaders' promise to them was kept.*
>
> Joshua 9:21

---

[28] Dave Butts, *The Sin of Prayerlessness,* https://www.harvestprayer.com/resources/personal-2/sin-of-prayerlessness/ accessed March 20, 2022.

Betrayal

The Israelites didn't kill them or break their word—instead, they used the Gibeonites to hew wood for the altar fire and draw water for the cleansing ritual of the temple. A sneak attack by the enemy was turned into a victory. The people who used deception to get their way were now forever consigned to serving the people of God.

The enemy tried his best to stop Joshua and his army from conquering Canaan, but he failed miserably. If you find yourself in a similar situation, don't give up, Confess the failure to God—receive His forgiveness—and move forward in victory!

10

Amy's Story

Rejection began in my life before I was even born. I was told all of my life that my oldest sister, who was a senior in High School when I was born, resented my mother and me for "ruining her life." Kathy was the Homecoming Queen, most popular cheerleader, most likely to succeed beloved girl in DeWitt High School. Now in the midst of her senior year, her mom was embarrassingly big and pregnant at her graduation. She once asked, "What are we going to do with it if it's ugly?" to which my mother replied, "Keep it just like I did you and Mitch."

To make matters worse, my mother went into labor on Kathy's birthday, July 2, 1967. It was the first year that Daylight Savings Time had been introduced. And thank God it was, because I was born at 12:10 AM on July 3, 1967. Even so, I felt I spent my entire life in the shadow of Kathy's birthday. On my sixteenth birthday I got a car, but that same year so did she. On her fiftieth birthday I was told by my mother that I was not having a birthday that year because it was Kathy's year to turn the big half a century and that my turn would come when I turned 50.

This constant rejection of having to live in my sister's shadow and being reminded that I ruined her life has been a very difficult thing to overcome. However, I must say that I never knew until later in life that

Betrayal

Kathy didn't feel towards me the way I had been led to believe. She shared with me that after I was born, she would put me in her car and parade me around town to show everyone her "beautiful baby sister." It is true, regardless of my early perception of mine and Kathy's relationship, and despite the fact that through most of our adult lives we were pulled by life in different directions, since going into ministry Kathy has become my best friend and biggest supporter. We have the closest, most amazing relationship I could ever hope for. She has become the best big sister ever! I thank God every day for giving us back the years that we missed, and I love and cherish her more than ever. Her only flaw is that she thinks Dwain is a saint who is perfect in all things! To which I just smile and say, "Yes, he is pretty perfect!"

I also had to live in my older brother Mitch's shadow because he became a very successful musician and minister. Everywhere I turned it seemed people were asking, "Do you play piano and sing like Mitch?" Not to mention the fact that Mother idolized him. We all did. As I have aged I realize that his approval for me was something I not only sought but needed my whole life. Living through these and other events that, you will soon learn, has made it very difficult for me to develop my own personal identity. It turned me into a non-confrontational people pleaser who would do "anything to just keep the peace." I was so starved for positive attention from my mother that I made sure the house was clean and her coffee was made when she got home from work every day. I would do anything to feel that she approved of me. I felt so average because I was medium height, medium build with medium brown hair that it made me want to change the spelling of my name in the sixth grade to Amie just to be unique somehow.

My earliest memory of my father, "Little Son," was when he would leave his car lot at 10:00 AM every morning and bring me a honey bun from the store. He always referred to me as his, "Pride and Joy." He loved to tease me by driving by leaving me crying in the driveway waiting on my honey bun. Then he would circle the block and pull in and share the morning with me. My father was a very good man that was loved by the entire town. However, he was a severe alcoholic. I have memories of my little two-and-a-half-year-old brother John and I jumping on the bed outside the bathroom crying in terror as we listened to dad vomiting up blood in the bathroom from his bleeding ulcers while my mom cried and held his head. He would disappear into his bedroom for weeks at a time and binge drink whiskey until he nearly died. When he ran out of liquor, he would dry out with help from my uncle and mom, then he would go back to work. On December 22, 1972, my little world came crashing down. I watched my sixteen year old brother, Mitch, pick my dad up and lay him in the back seat of our car and drive him and mom to Little Rock to Baptist Hospital where, on Christmas Day, he had his first of several surgeries to repair his bleeding ulcers. My final memory of my father was when he called me on the phone from the hospital. Realizing he was dying, he was too emotional to say anything to me. I just heard him sobbing on the other end of the line as he handed the phone to my mother. My father was only 43 when he passed away. The entire town of DeWitt, Arkansas closed down due to a mayoral proclamation to honor him on the day of his funeral. That may seem foreign to many, but that's just what the wonderful people of our small southern town would do when a public figure died. I must say how proud I am to be from DeWitt, Arkansas. That place and those wonderful people have a very special place in my heart. Today it is still the most wonderful community in the world.

The one ray of hope in all of this is that Brother Jerry Miller, our pastor and Dwain's dad, led my dad to the Lord two weeks before he died. I will never forget Brother Jerry coming to our house to tell me that my daddy went to heaven. He made it sound like Daddy went to Disneyland! He was so good at comforting me that I never truly dealt with my dad's death until I was 35 years old. I was on my way to visit my brother Mitch when I began to cry so hard over my father that I had to pull off of the interstate. I realized that I had to give my father permission to have left me. I said, "Daddy, it's ok that you died and I will see you again because Brother Jerry said I would."

Betrayal

I will never forget a very special moment much later in life with my mom. I told her that "Pomp and Circumstance" always made me cry. She told me it was because I associated it with daddy's death because right after he died, I graduated kindergarten.

After my father's death, my brother Mitch stepped up at sixteen and became a tremendous father figure in mine and my little brother John's life. I have such admiration and respect for him and the stability he brought to our family and still does to this day.

However, there is no way to know how deep of an impact losing my father at age five had on my life. I had a huge hole in my heart that I realized later in life was the source of many bad decisions I made in regards to relationships. I just wanted to be loved. I just wanted a man to be proud of me the way that my daddy was.

After my father passed away, it left mom with four children, three at home, having to find a way to provide on just a tenth grade education. I found great comfort in my little brother. We all affectionately called him "John John." I was able to be a sort of caretaker in his life, and at the same time he unknowingly was giving me emotional support that I didn't even realize I needed at the time. Growing up and feeling responsible for John was not a burden. As a matter of fact, to this day he is still a rock in my life that I lean on. I will be forever grateful for this very special relationship that he and I have. I love Kathy and Mitch, but they left home when we were little because Mom had us later in life. This caused John and I to develop a very special and close bond to this day. He uses his wonderful sense of humor to cheer me up when I need to laugh the most. He is one of the funniest people I know, and he dances really well too! My memories of John and I growing up together are the one area of my childhood that makes me smile.

After my father died, my childhood was filled with turmoil, drama and instability. I remember a night when a person came into my bedroom to confront my mom, who was sleeping with me. A gun was pointed at my mother and me. I ran and got my older brother Mitch,

Amy's Story

who fortunately was visiting that night. He came into the room and defused the situation. We grabbed what we could and got into our car. Mitch drove us around all night long until it was safe to go back home and gather our things.

On the heels of this upheaval in my life, I found myself being sexual abused by a man old enough to be my father. This began at age nine and lasted for three years. At the age of nine, I guess I didn't have the ability to process that it was abuse. I felt I had done something so wrong, and then my mother validated my feelings when her response to the abuse was, "Miss Amy, what did you do to provoke this?"

This event caused my mother to be suspicious of me my entire life. She accused me often of trying to provoke men. I am not speaking ill of my mother. I realize that she did the best she could with the hand she had been dealt in life. She was a survivor who always told me, "Miss Amy, you just have to pull yourself up by your boot straps, hold your head high, stand up, straighten up, put your shoulders back, suck in your stomach and move forward." She grew up basically without a father, had to work as a telephone operator at age eleven and only completed the tenth grade. Looking back, I know how tough she was, and she wanted me to be tough too. She was a part of that generation that just didn't show weakness nor allowed anyone else to. Everything was swept under the rug. No one was allowed speak of problems or say anything negative. That was just that generation.

To say that this drove me into a bad place is an understatement. I know now, after going through deliverance for all of this, that a spirit of perversion was attached to me as a result of being abused. This resulted in grown men trying to put their hands on me all of my adolescent years. Then, even in early adulthood while I was single, I was raped on two separate occasions. I thought it was normal and somehow I must deserve it or cause it because that's what my mother told me when I was twelve. As an adult, I had men constantly coming after me, and because of the hole in my heart left by my father's death I just wanted attention. So, I made many bad choices in my young life, and the desire for true love and acceptance became more unattainable. Thankfully, God sent a pastor and his wife into my life that knew about deliverance ministry, and I was able to break this familiar spirit and all of those soul ties off of my life and begin to heal from all of the abuse.

At age 14, my mother and Mitch, who was my father figure, agreed that it would be acceptable for me to begin dating a 20 year old man who had been our neighbor and was involved in our church. I allowed him to be very controlling over me. I lost all of my High School years because I allowed him to control me. He told me I couldn't be a cheerleader; told me how to wear my hair; who my friends could be; and actually didn't allow me to have any friends. Like I said, I had a huge hole in my heart and just wanted to be loved. He and I broke up before my senior year. I had the best year of my life, finally being a cheerleader and having friends. The best day of my life was when I was selected to Homecoming Court and my mom took off work to spend the entire day with me. I finally felt love and acceptance from my mom for one day.

Unfortunately, he and I got back together because I felt I had no other option for security. I married him right after I graduated High School. I was seventeen years old. We were divorced within two years.

A few years after my divorce, I met the man who would become the father of my daughter. I truly married him because I thought I loved him. However, he was a typical South Arkansas man who focused his life on work, hunting and fishing, which left me with a continued emptiness inside. I just wanted to be noticed. I just wanted to be someone's number one. So, I continued to make decisions that were not healthy.

Six years in to our marriage, our beautiful little Kelsea Marie was born. I named her after the one truly supportive adult in my life, my Aunt Winifred Marie. She was my rock all of my life until she passed away in 1998.

Amy's Story

Kelsea and I had a phenomenal relationship. Looking back at some old video footage, she and I were inseparable. However, due to some poor choices on my part, her father and I divorced right before she turned five. I take full responsibility for this failed marriage. I lay no blame on anyone but myself. This would prove to put a whole lot of strain on mine and Kelsea's relationship. Right after the divorce, things were good. Unfortunately they did not remain that way. I remarried and that put her in a difficult place. Again, as a result of choices that I made and other influences beyond my control, she and I have not had a relationship since she was twelve years old. This has proven to be the hardest and most painful experience of my life. God did use Kelsea to bring some perspective and healing into my life. One day at church when she was nine years old I saw her standing in the altar with her friends and it dawned on me that she was the age I was when I was molested. God spoke to me and revealed that there is no way a nine year old girl could provoke a man old enough to be her father into an inappropriate relationship with her. That day I began to forgive myself realizing I did not cause the abuse.

I can remember one day in particular. I was dealing with depression and suicidal thoughts caused by not having Kelsea in my life. I cried out to God for help. As I pulled out on the highway, Holy Spirit spoke to me. He said, "Do you see that large open field of flowers?"

I replied, "yes."

He said, "I planted those just for you! That's how much I love you Amy."

Along the way, God has given me little love letters and signs to let me know that He has me and this whole situation in His hands. I know that one day, even if it is in heaven, Kelsea Marie will be restored to me.

My prayer has always been, "My God don't let me go through this and not use this to help someone else." I have learned that you cannot control someone else's decisions or actions. But, if you continue to praise God in the midst of your storm, He will give you the faith to pull you through. This is the reason I share my story. Not to garner attention, sympathy or make excuses for my poor decisions in life. I share all of this with you hoping and praying that my story can help someone else who knows the pain of rejection, abandonment, abuse and loss. If I can live by God's grace without being a victim, so can you!

The greatest struggle of my life has been having the ability to forgive myself. I would forgive myself and then something would happen and I would go around the blame mountain again. I know in my heart that God has forgiven me. I know that I have forgiven myself. I know that God has given me the man that I have always prayed for and dreamed of. The Lord has restored so much in my life. Dwain's family has embraced me unconditionally. His Dad, Brother Jerry, who told me about my father going to heaven, called me his daughter-in-law recently and my heart jumped for joy. Unfortunately, our relationship was cut way too short when the Lord promoted him to heaven in the fall of 2020.

I know that my mother and father who are with the Lord in heaven are looking down with great approval of the woman I have become. I have received a lot of help in the healing process to become who I am today, but the day I decided to love myself is the day I started living again. You must love yourself. The greatest form of betrayal is to betray your own heart by denying it the love and acceptance that God placed within you for yourself. Without that, you are no good to Him or anyone else.

In the end, my prayer is being answered. I am finally at a place where God is using me and my story in ministry to help so many others. Thank you Jesus! I am that conduit that I prayed to be when I was twelve years old. You are using me to pour out your love on others.

Apostle Clay Nash confirmed for me three years ago in a meeting through a prophetic word that this was what I was created to do. He

Amy's Story

saw me at five years old standing by a tree next to our house. He reminded me of my first encounter with God and prophesied to me that I had finally come into the purpose that God had promised me when I was five. He also shared that the enemy had done all that he could to keep me from reaching this place in life but that I had in fact made it!

Don't give up! It's never too late. I like to say, "God's promises have no expiration date!"

I end my story with my life's verse, Jeremiah 29:11.

For I know the plans I have for you," declares the Lord, "plans to prosper you and not to harm you, plans to give you a hope and a future.

11

Dwain's Story

HOW TO OVERCOME SELF-BETRAYAL AND LIVE IN FREEDOM!

We sometimes get offended by God and scandalized because He allows us to go through some stuff!

I've been there!!!!!

I can tell you from personal experience that there have been many times that I felt betrayed by the Father over the past 37 years of ministry. I had nights when I cried all night long. I looked up to heaven and told the Father that I was ticked off. I declared that I have thrown in the towel, only to have Him throw it back.

I will never forget when I transitioned our church from a traditional denominational congregationally ruled body to becoming an interdenominational Spirit-filled church with an Apostolic covering. We endured three mass exoduses in ten years.

The first exodus came because I preached too much on the crucifixion and the blood atonement of Jesus. My sermons were deemed too graphic for some of the elite members of the church. We lost five thousand dollars in income per week in the church when the white-collar members pulled out. I was only 29 years old at the time.

Betrayal

Thank God for Dr. Ron Phillips and Dr. Tod Zeiger and their wisdom. They had been through a similar situation a decade earlier in their churches. During this walk-out, I attended the inaugural Fresh Oil and New Wine conference at Dr. Phillips's church in Chattanooga. In that meeting, I heard the testimony of Dr. Phillips and how God sustained them in the face of total financial ruin—it encouraged me greatly to stay the course and not run. Dr. Tod Zeiger was teaching every morning that week about his journey and the betrayal he had endured. His messages set my heart free from the ministry's performance trap. One morning he was preaching up a storm about, "What we see as disaster and ruin, God sees as liberating us to be who and what He created us to be and no longer having to answer to a system and having to please some board." The message got a hold of me. Before I knew what had happened, I took a lap around the sanctuary! Thank God for wise counsel during these seasons of betrayal that puts the actions of the Father into perspective. By the grace of God, we survived that season of the financial crisis. On paper, I still can't explain it. But isn't that how God works?

The second exodus occurred over the sacred cow of worship style. Someone once said, "When Lucifer, the worship leader of heaven was kicked out, he landed in the church's choir loft!" That statement is more accurate than you think. My staff and I were called to a big deacon meeting one night. When I say big, there were about 35 deacons present. They began to blast my new, young worship pastor. I stopped them and assured them that their problem was with me because he followed my direction. They wanted to know why we had to sing off of a screen, why couldn't we sing out of a hymnal anymore, why the choir stopped wearing choir robes, and of course, why in the world did the music have to be so loud? Then the real truth came out. They sat and attacked me for two hours about transitioning the church into one of those holy roller churches, making us the town's laughingstock. Never mind that they had witnessed more signs, wonders, and miracles and more people being born again than all the churches' previous eighty-plus years combined. The greatest betrayal is that not one of my younger deacons—who were my spiritual sons—defended me. As a result of this meeting and my refusal to change the music, a large contingency left the church, and unfortunately, so did my young staff, and I didn't blame them.

I thought, boy, I will show them because a church of 3,000 was talking to me about being their pastor.

When I walked out of that meeting that night Holy Spirit said to me, "You are no longer the pastor of this church."

I responded, "Good, I don't want to be the pastor of this church, so get me out of here."

Then, the following week the chairman of the search committee of that big church came to see me crying, telling me that I would not be coming to pastor their church because one older man on the committee's wife didn't like my sermon. I was devastated. For one solid year, Holy Spirit was absent from our church. I was so depressed, hurt, and betrayed that I would wait until the music began and walk into the service, sit on the front pew, preach, then walk out and go home without greeting anyone. I was angry at God, and I wanted everyone to know it. Fortunately, those young deacons began to seek God in prayer and repented of their lack of defense of me, and then revival broke out!

The Holy Spirit told me, "Since the large church missed Me, I will give you what they were supposed to have." And He did. Our church grew by leaps and bounds. We experienced the outpouring of the Holy Spirit as I had only seen in the great revival at Brownsville Assembly of God in 1996.

We reached the people that no one else in our city wanted. We witnessed hundreds of people being saved and delivered from addiction. Ministries were birthed, and ministers were raised up and sent out. We had become a Book of Acts church.

The third exodus occurred when Holy Spirit told me to change the church's name. I was threatened, lied about, and called everything you can imagine, but those not-so-young deacons defended me this time. They removed a man who charged at me in the meeting and was going to hit me. I agreed that if we didn't get an 85 percent approval from the congregation to change the name, then we would leave it as Second Baptist Church. But, if we received at least 85 percent, we would change the name to Cross Life Church. As the Holy Spirit would have it, 75 to 100 members (most of whom had been members there for more than 50 years) would exit out of their frustration months before the vote. They said, "We will take our money, and he will go under." Well, the vote passed by 86 percent. If they had stayed, they would have outvoted me! Over the next six months, the church grew by 300 people. To God be the glory, I can tell you that from 2006 until 2016, that church was in one of the greatest outpourings in America.

During the most challenging days of these 37 years of ministry, when people were lying, forsaking, mocking, abandoning, and closing doors for bigger and better opportunities, I became very bitter, cynical, cold, and hurt! There was a time when I was the most cynical pastor I'd ever known. I had people walk out of my life that I had invested in for two decades. Yes, I took it personally. I am not proud of that, but thanks to the grace of our merciful God, He brought me out of it.

I had learned that if God had given me what I had asked for when I was walking through these challenging times, it would have destroyed me. God always gives us what our maturity level can handle at the time and thank God He does.

The greatest challenge for those in ministry is not to take the enemy's bait when it comes to being offended at God for hurts, pains, wounds, and noes to your prayers!

It's hard to handle when God says NO!

We have to be like Jesus and Stephen when they were being martyred: Father, forgive them! Which also when translated means I forgive You too.

Dwain's Story

I had a lady become offended at a message I preached one Sunday and leave my church because I led people in prayer and said, "God, I forgive you!" She was so spiritual she'd never been angry at or blamed God for anything. Well, for us real folks, I can say I have had to forgive God many times. I like to think He looks at me and laughs and says, "Yes, my Son died for that too."

But the greatest betrayal was that I betrayed MYSELF!

I thought I was too important—certain things and people and opportunities were beneath me!

So, what did I do?

- I isolated myself and became privileged.

> *A man who isolates himself seeks his own desire;*
> *He rages against all wise judgment.*
>
> Proverbs 18:1 (NKJV)

- I thought I was untouchable to the enemy, and I wouldn't listen to anyone. I remember Dr. Randy Caldwell told me what was coming, and I still wouldn't listen.

> *A fool has no delight in understanding,*
> *But in expressing his own heart.*
>
> Proverbs 18:2 (NKJV)

- I ignored the red flags of the Holy Spirit and Word.
- Things were being said, taught, and actions of manipulation were being justified by myself and others I was with, and I thought the end justified the means.
- I was deceived by greed, pride, and power and it cost me everything.
- I wanted the money to give away, but for my name's sake.

Betrayal

> *Choose a good reputation over great riches;*
> *being held in high esteem is better than silver or gold.*
> *The rich and poor have this in common:*
> *The Lord made them both.*
> *A prudent person foresees danger and takes precautions.*
> *The simpleton goes blindly on and suffers the consequences.*
> *True humility and fear of the Lord*
> *lead to riches, honor, and long life.*
>
> Proverbs 22:1-4 (NLT)

In the end, I was guilty of betraying my own heart.

I take full responsibility for the choices I've made in my life. In the end, God has taught me a lot about myself. Before my beautiful wife, Amy, passed, she would tell me on numerous occasions, "I didn't like the Dwain you were when you were around the big shot preachers and when you ministered in these big venues. But I do like this Dwain, who has become humble, grateful, and approachable."

The application of this book on Betrayal is not to give any of us permission to hold on to grudges, think about getting even, or even pray for bad things to happen to those who betrayed us. It is designed to help you and me understand that you are not alone. Betrayal is a fact of life. All of us will be betrayed at some level by someone sooner or later. In the end, as long as we don't betray ourselves by allowing our feelings or our flesh to get involved, we will survive and become much better from the experience.

The hardest thing for me to do in all of this was first; to take ownership of my arrogance and attitude of privilege, then second, to forgive myself and believe that the Father would restore someone who had become so self-centered and self-serving. I cannot tell you how repentant I am for all the manipulation I participated in, in the Name of Jesus! What I preached then was the truth, and it still is. But the way that I prostituted the Gospel justifying the means for the end, is what I am truly sorry for. A lot of innocent people were hurt in the process and for that, I am deeply sorry.

Yes, I have been betrayed, like David, at the deepest level possible. However, I became what was done to me. Let that sink in. I became what was done to me. And that was the greatest betrayal of all. I betrayed myself.

I discovered the key to not living in the betrayal and being able to forgive and move on is in the following:

1. Have a funeral for your past (read Philippians 3:13).
2. Take control of your thoughts (read Philippians 4:8 in the AMP).
3. Get a vision for your life through your God-given imagination. Ask God for divine downloads of the Holy Spirit.

God is not through with you. You must refuse to allow who you were yesterday to define you today!

Remember, to quote Pastor Steve McCuin, "The only way the devil wins, or you fail, is for you to quit doing what God created you to do!"

After all, David was an adulterer and a murderer and God called him, "A man after my own heart." How is that possible? Because David, even though he betrayed Himself, owned it, repented, and accepted the consequences of his actions. And you can too.

I truly believe because I took ownership of my failures and feelings, refused to blame others, and take up a spirit of offense, God has and is fully restoring all things in my life. The key to the comeback in your life is within you.

When Amy died, I know some religious zealots spoke out that this was God's judgment upon us. However, I prayed and said, "Father, forgive them for they truly know not what they do." And I meant it!

There is much ignorance in the body of Christ concerning the heart of the Father. His grace and mercy extend toward us all, with no exceptions. I have vowed to live my life in total love, acceptance, and forgiveness toward others no matter their failure or behavior towards me or others.

The seed of restoration comes to those whose heart is prepared to receive it. Brokenness or bitterness is the fruit of life's most devastating blows. We will all face the tragedy of betrayal. For a short time, I felt more betrayed than ever when Amy died. I was angry, hurt, disillusioned, depressed, and despondent, and I prayed to die. However, through a series of supernatural encounters, the Father tilled the soil of my heart with His love, grace, and mercy, and my heart became one of gratitude and praise. It was at that moment restoration began. It began with deliverance and then divine destiny when the Father sent sweet Cameron into my life. She is my miracle of restoration.

The next book you read from me will include her and we will share our story. It is truly mind-blowing and miraculous.

I want you to know that no matter what you've done, or been through if you allow the Holy Spirit to keep your heart out of the pit of betrayal… **IT AIN'T OVER!**

Made in the USA
Middletown, DE
23 October 2022